THE LANGUAGE OF
DRAWING AND PAINTING

THE LANGUAGE OF DRAWING AND PAINTING

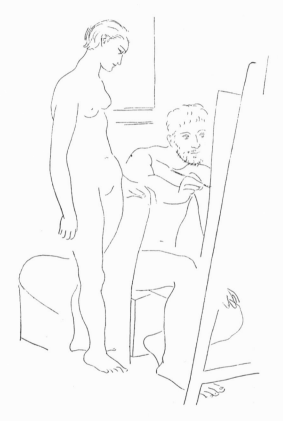

by Arthur Pope

NEW YORK / RUSSELL & RUSSELL

*The "Artist and Model" on the title page
is a reproduction of an etching by Picasso*

PREFATORY NOTE TO THE NEW EDITION

In order to lower costs, this edition is printed without the color plates, or charts, of earlier editions. Instead, it is assumed that the serious student for whom the book is primarily intended will produce his own fundamental charts or scales—almost a necessary procedure in any case, since references to the charts are made in the text, if one is to obtain a clear understanding of the subject of color (or visual tone). Directions for the execution of these scales, or charts, are given in the text accompanying Figs. 1, 2, 3, 5, and 11. These are referred to as:

Color Chart   I   Scale of Values (retained in this edition as Plate LXVI)

Color Chart   II   Scale of Hues

Color Chart III   Scale of Intensities

Color Chart IV   Scale of Values and Intensities of Single Hue

Color Chart   V   Scale of Highest Intensities of Twelve Hues at Seven Value Levels (to economize in time and labor the hues might be limited to six main [one-letter] hues)

PREFACE

The present book is a revision and rearrangement of my two earlier books, *The Painter's Terms* and *The Painter's Modes of Expression*, with the addition of a certain amount of new material, in particular that dealing with visual perception and visual concepts. The books mentioned were originally planned to form the first two volumes in a series to be called *An Introduction to the Language of Drawing and Painting*, later volumes of which were to deal with pictorial design and with the materials and procedures of painting. As it seemed wise to change the terminology employed in the books so far published to bring it more into line with more usual terminologies and especially with that recently proposed by the Colorimetry Committee of the Optical Society of America, I have thought it best to revise the two earlier volumes in one volume and to leave the problem of pictorial design for a separate book. The subject of materials and methods has been fairly adequately treated by other authors and discussion of this matter may well be left in other hands.

The principal change in terminology consists in the substitution of the term *hue* for that of *color* in the more specific sense. This is common usage. This allows for the use of the term *color* in the more general sense of "opposed to neutral" or what is sometimes called *chromatic* tone or color as opposed to *achromatic* tone or color. At the same time, however, I have adhered to the use of the term *value* in place of the Colorimetry Committee's *brightness* (or *lightness*) and of *tone* in place of *color* as used by scientists in the more inclusive sense, as for our particular purposes less confusing and yet perfectly understandable to scientists. I have also adhered to the use of *intensity* (of hue) in place of *chroma* or *saturation* for similar reasons.

The aim of this book, as of those preceding on which it is based, is first of all to give an understanding of the principles underlying representation in the terms of drawing and painting so that the things themselves — the actual drawings and paintings — executed in a variety of ways and for varying purposes, may be understood. From this point of view we are dealing with a language or rather with a number of different languages which, like those spoken or written, must first be understood.

A further aim is to give a sound basis for critical judgment. Much vagueness in the criticism of painting, for example, has been due to the fact that until comparatively recently the general theory of visual perception as well as the theory of color or tone relations has been imperfectly understood. At best it is a complicated subject and many problems still remain to be worked out; but in the last few years much progress toward more precise concepts (physical, psychophysical, and psychological) and more widely accepted terminologies has been made by groups like the Colorimetry Committee of the O. S. A. and by persons carrying on investigations in various scientific laboratories. The point of view of the artist and of the discriminating patron may be very different from that of the scientific worker; nevertheless any sound basic theory of tone or color in the arts, no matter how different the particular application, must conform to sound scientific concepts, and in order to understand the use of tone or color in painting it is necessary in the first place to have some clear ideas about it.

The classification of the different factors (or attributes) involved in tone or color which is used in this book is based on that proposed some forty and more years ago by Denman W. Ross and published in his various books, reference to which will be found in the text. I have put this into three-dimensional form, which I speak of as the *working tone solid*. Here we run immediately into the distinction between the point of view of the scientist and the practical necessity of the artist. To the modern scientific worker used to precise specification by means of an electric eye in a mechanical colorimeter, this working solid may seem like a woeful distortion. It is in fact a rough-and-ready approximation. Nevertheless, for the practice of painting and especially for introductory teaching purposes in connection with the theory of tone or color it has distinct advantages. In the actual practice of painting the artist must necessarily base his handling of pigment mixtures (differing from mixtures of light) to some extent on approximations, and he must have some system of classification that is easily workable. At the same time, if he has a clear understanding of the limitations of his practice and has a definite concept of what a true tone solid would be like, he can carry his visual discrimination to any degree of refinement that he

chooses. Moreover, for certain purposes he may turn to other classifications, and when the true tone solid based on accurate visual intervals
is finally produced he may use it for special problems for which it is
appropriate. However, even the true tone solid will not render the
working solid for its particular purposes at all useless or obsolete.

It has not seemed necessary to deal at length with the physics of
light or the general physiology and psychology of vision, for there are
many books devoted to these still imperfectly understood matters to
which the reader may easily refer. I have attempted, however, to show
the relation of the terminology and the classification used in this book
to other terminologies and other classifications. I have also dealt briefly
with the difference between additive and subtractive mixing and with
the difference between a true tone solid and the approximate solid
devised here for practical purposes. Furthermore I have tried to show
the difference between the factors of *value* and *intensity* (*chroma*)
and the entirely distinct factors sometimes called by scientific writers
brightness and *saturation* and herein to avoid confusion called *brilliance*
and *purity*, for a great deal of confused thinking has resulted from the
failure to distinguish between these two sets of factors. For example,
intensity (or chroma) and saturation are often treated as equivalent
terms, and they may of course be so used; but saturation is also often
used in a sense that is not at all identical with that of intensity or
chroma, as these terms are ordinarily defined. There is often the same
confusion in the use of the term brightness. The fact that so many
people almost instinctively speak of tints and shades is indication that
there is visual significance in the distinction between the two sets of
factors.

It may seem rather absurd at first to suggest that a painter or a
student of painting, to say nothing of the general public, should spend
a lot of time trying to understand the rather complicated theory of
color or tone relations. But drawing and painting as visual arts deal
primarily with the terms of vision. A knowledge of these terms and of
the possibilities of their arrangement in the art of drawing and painting
is fundamental to a complete understanding of the subject. As suggested above, ignorance in this respect is responsible for much vagueness in criticism, and also for much gushing sentimentality in what
usually goes under the title of appreciation. As for practice, one may

feel very sure that the great painters of the past have known fairly well what they were about. Their knowledge, however, was a matter of workshop tradition; it was acquired slowly by experimental practice, and handed on from master to apprentice for generation after generation. This empirical knowledge based on tradition has been largely lost; and the workshop method of training which fostered it cannot be recovered under present conditions, even if it should be desirable. Knowledge of a similar nature can be obtained at the present time only by means of a study of fundamental principles. Unfortunately there is a popular fear that knowledge may destroy originality and imagination. It has not done so in the past, for the greatest artists, although mostly not such extreme theorists as Leonardo, have yet given much careful thought to the materials and procedures and the general aims of their craft. There is really no reason why a prospective artist should not know something definite about the terms of the art with which he is going to express his ideas so that his painting may be conducted on an intelligent and sensible basis.

Today we have the whole art of the world spread before us as a source of inspiration. When this is looked at without understanding of the varied cultural environments or of the principles of expression involved, there is little wonder that the result is often a mere clumsy counterfeiting of the superficial aspect of some so-called primitive or provincial art, or a vague attempt to produce something that will look as startlingly strange as some of these things which we seem to admire. It takes intelligence to apply the fundamental principles to be discovered in the varied art of the past to the problems of our own time; and this must be based on understanding on the part of the artist on the one hand, and on the part of the patron on the other. It has always been intelligence on both sides of this twofold partnership of artist and patron that has produced the great art of the past, and it is only the same sort of intelligence that can produce art of genuine significance at the present day. The art of the past has been largely a matter of rather narrow tradition — a concentrated study of the use of a limited range of materials and terms. The art of the present day must inevitably be based on a broad eclecticism — a rational eclecticism, I should like to call it. For this, a sound theoretical basis is a necessity.

I like to think of what I have written not as the expression of a merely personal point of view but rather as the product of studies concerning the art of drawing and painting which have been carried out during the last fifty or sixty years by a succession of teachers and students in the Department of Fine Arts of Harvard University. It has been the aim of these studies to build up a body of knowledge to form the basis for a genuine theory of the visual arts comparable to theory in music, understanding of which is taken for granted for the intelligent listener as well as for the composer and performer. In the visual arts there has been history on the one hand and practice on the other, with theory (partly on account of the complications of the general subject of vision) largely neglected. It is not, to be sure, that plenty of "theories" have not been propounded in the last few years so that one hesitates to use the word; but these "theories" have usually been personal affairs devised by those who, as T. M. Greene remarks, "for this task are not always ideally equipped." It is hoped that this book may prove at least a helpful contribution toward a sound theory of the art of drawing and painting removed as far as possible from personal prejudice.

It is evident that to give credit for many of the ideas embodied in such a book as this or in many cases even to realize their source is quite impossible. Tradition in scholarship is much like that in art; one's original contribution, though it may have its special value, is often relatively small. If the present result is of value, credit must be given first to my early teachers, Charles Herbert Moore, Martin Mower, and Denman W. Ross, and then to a host of colleagues and students by whose friendly counsel I have profited, and especially those who at one time or another have acted as my assistants and have since gone on to more important posts in colleges and museums. I pay grateful tribute to them all. For much wise advice and sympathetic understanding in connection with the present volume I am especially indebted to Morton C. Bradley, Jr., James M. Carpenter, and Jakob Rosenberg.

To many persons and organizations I am under grateful obligation for permission to reproduce photographs or other material. Individual acknowledgments will be found in the legends accompanying the figures and plates.

A. P.

Fogg Art Museum, January 1949

CONTENTS

PLATES

PART ONE

THE TERMS OF
DRAWING AND PAINTING

I

THE TERMS OF VISION AND OF DRAWING AND PAINTING · THE WORKING TONE SOLID

THE VISUAL IMAGE

When we say that we see objects existing in space, what actually happens is that objects are projected upon the retina of the eye by rays of light traveling from the objects to the eye. This projection on the retina of the eye — the primary basis for visual experience, which has to be transformed into sensation, and then ordinarily interpreted by the mind into the facts of existence, before what we think of as seeing occurs — is a two-dimensional image (the visual image) and corresponds to a cross section of the cone of rays of light converging on the eye. It is like the image formed on the ground-glass plate of a camera. The visual image is composed of areas distinguished from each other by differences in quantity and quality of light.[1] These areas may be placed high or low, to the right or to the left in the field of vision in relation to its center; they may be large or small in relation to other areas; they may be round, or square, or oval, or some other shape — that is, they may vary in *position*,[2] *measure*, and *shape*. These areas may also be light or dark; they may be red or yellow or green or blue, or some intermediate hue, or they may be neutral gray; they may be strong in red or yellow or some other hue, or they may be weak in hue — grayish. In other words, if we use the term *value* to indicate the degree of lightness or darkness, the term *hue* to indicate the quality due to the predominance of some one of the wave lengths which make

[1] For the whole process of vision, for which the light acts as an external stimulus, see "The Concept of Color, Chapter II of the forthcoming Colorimetry Report," Journal of the Optical Society of America, Vol. 33, No. 10 (October, 1943); also R. M. Evans, *An Introduction to Color* (New York: Wiley, 1948).

[2] Position in this sense indicates *location*. Under position must also be included the *attitude* of a given area, that is, the direction of its main axis in relation to the vertical and horizontal, and also *interval*, that is, the distance between it and other areas. However, we are not concerned with these factors for the present.

up white light, and the term *intensity* to indicate the strength of the
hue as distinguished from neutrality, we may say that these areas vary
in *value*, *hue*, and *hue-intensity*. The term *tone* may be used in a
general way to include these three factors of *value*, *hue*, and *intensity*;
and we may say that the visual image is made up of areas varying in
tone (that is, in *value*, *hue*, and *intensity*) and arranged in different
positions, *measures*, and *shapes*. We may define the visual image by
defining the position, the measure, the shape, and the tone of each of its
areas. We define the tone of an area by defining its value, its hue, and
its intensity; or in the case of a neutral, like white or black or an intermediate gray, which is at the zero point of intensity and hence has no
hue, by defining its value.

The term *color* may be used to indicate a tone which is other than
neutral, that is, distinguished from neutral by a given intensity of a
given hue. Thus, as in much everyday speech, we may speak of colored
tones as opposed to neutral tones. Colored tones are sometimes called
chromatic as opposed to achromatic. Colored tones, or simply colors,
are distinguished from each other by differences of value, hue, and
intensity; neutral (or uncolored) tones are distinguished by differences
of value only.[3]

To sum up, the terms of vision are as follows:

Visual Areas (or Visual Tones) distinguished by differences in

   (I) the spatial factors (or attributes)

          position (location, attitude, interval)

          measure (or size)

          shape

  (II) the tonal factors (or attributes)

          value

          hue   ⎫

                  ⎬color

          intensity⎭

          to which may be added the factors or attributes of

          purity and brilliance, explained in the next chapter.

    [3] We might speak of the areas which make up the visual image as *visual tones*,
using the term as somewhat analogous to tone in sound. These are distinguished
from auditual tones in that they are produced by light waves instead of sound
waves, and that they have extension in two dimensions in space instead of in time.
We might say then that the visual image is made up of visual tones (or simply
tones) varying in value, hue, and intensity, and arranged in different positions,

THE TERMS OF DRAWING AND PAINTING

With pigment materials spread on a flat surface such as paper or canvas, we may produce areas which, like those composing the visual image, have extension in two dimensions.[4] We may make these areas light or dark; we may make them red or yellow, or some other hue; and we may make them strong in that hue, or weak, or neutral gray.

---

measures, and shapes. We may thus speak of the areas of the visual image as visual tones; or we may speak of the tone of an area; or we may speak of a tone of a given value, hue, and intensity in the abstract, regardless of the limitation of measure, shape, and position; and we may speak of the general tonality of a group of areas, if they approach each other closely in value, hue, and intensity. These uses of the term *tone* are convenient, consistent, and, I believe, easily understood.

Other words are often used in place of those defined above, and the same words are frequently used in other meanings, often very vaguely. It must be borne in mind that it does not much matter what words we use, so long as we define them clearly and use them consistently to express the different factors involved. An explanation of some of the variations in terminology, however, will perhaps make these as well as the one used in this book more easily understood. Thus the term *color* is often used to mean a specific tone, including neutrals from black to white as well as those possessing specific hues and intensities. The scientist generally uses the term *color* in this way as the equivalent of tone as defined above. (See A. H. Munsell, *A Color Notation*, Boston, 1905; or *The Munsell Book of Color*, Munsell Color Co., Inc., Baltimore, 1929; or the Optical Society's *The Concept of Color*, op. cit.) Also, in everyday speech it is often said that the color of a house is white, or the color of a dress gray or black. At other times color is often used to distinguish a tone as differing from gray or neutral — for instance a "movie" in color as opposed to one in black and white. For our particular purposes I believe the term *tone* as the inclusive term, in place of color as used in scientific writing, is less confusing. We shall accordingly leave the term *color* to be used in the more vague fashion of ordinary speech, or we shall use it occasionally in the sense of "opposed to neutral" when it is convenient and the meaning is perfectly clear.

Munsell uses the term *chroma* as the equivalent of intensity to denote strength of hue. *Saturation* is sometimes used in the same sense, but it is also sometimes used in a slightly different sense, as will be explained farther on. The terms *luminosity*, *brightness*, and *lightness* are sometimes used in place of value.

[4] For convenience in drawing and painting and especially in pure design, areas may be referred to as *dots*, *lines*, or *areas*, the last of which may be represented by *outlines* instead of by a distinction of tone from a background or adjacent areas. Dots represent locations which like mathematical points have no extension; but, as actually drawn or painted, dots may of course vary in size and tone, so they are merely small areas. Likewise lines as drawn or painted are actually areas having width as well as length although they may simply represent mathematical extension in one dimension. A straight line does represent such a mathematical extension but in the case of a curved or an angular line, there is always a suggestion of extension in width as well as length, and the factor of area shape immediately enters. Also, as we shall see is frequently the case, a line may even be drawn in such a way as to suggest three-dimensional form.

We may give these areas different positions, different measures, and different shapes. Thus, the terms of drawing and painting are like the terms of vision — *areas* (or *visual tones*) produced by pigment materials, varying in *value*, *hue*, and *intensity*, and arranged in different *positions*, *measures*, and *shapes*.

In all drawing and painting we are dealing in some way with these factors. Sometimes we may consider the arrangement of these factors only from the standpoint of the significance of their arrangement in two dimensions on the flat surface. In this we take the point of view of pure design, or what might better be called pure drawing and painting. We might at the same time use shapes of areas or lines which would suggest natural objects more or less. This might be for the interest or entertainment to be derived from the suggestion of representation, or for the sake of some symbolic significance attached to the objects suggested. Or it might be that we could obtain a greater amount of interest in the individual motives developed in the form of pattern by deriving them from natural forms than by trying to invent perfectly abstract motives. In this case the natural motive would be merely the starting point and would have to be adapted to the general intent of the pattern in a manner appropriate to the particular occasion. This has been done constantly by designers of brocades, textiles, pottery, and similar objects, in which the primary concern has been with the interest of surface pattern. The final excellence of the drawing or painting done from such a point of view must of course depend primarily on the character of the formal arrangement of the tones on the surface, with regard to positions, measures, and shapes, and values, hues, and intensities.

At the other extreme we might have an arrangement of these factors so ordered as to produce a definite expression of existence in space beyond the plane of the painting or drawing. This requires a definite organization of the spatial and tonal factors (regardless of mere surface pattern), which may have an aesthetic significance in itself. In between these two extremes we may have a great variety of types, some with more emphasis on surface pattern, others with greater emphasis on illusionistic representation (though usually not without regard to surface pattern at the same time), according to the function of the particular drawing or painting. But in all cases we are dealing with arrangements of the same terms or factors, and these are the same as the terms of vision.

TONE SCALES

In order to think and talk definitely of tone relations, we must make definite classifications or scales by which we may measure the different factors or elements in a tone; so, leaving aside for the present the question of positions, measures, and shapes, let us consider the possibilities in the way of the classification of tones with regard to value, hue, and intensity, and the expression of the relations of these factors by graphic diagrams. All such classifications are necessarily arbitrary, and an infinite number may be made, but the following scales first published many years ago by Denman W. Ross [5] are particularly useful in the actual practice of painting. These scales, as they may be produced by painting materials, are of course not scientifically accurate, but must be thought of as adjusted or tempered for the convenience of the painter. To cite only one instance, the white and black of painting are not perfect white and perfect black. The best white paint or white paper absorbs a certain proportion of rays of light falling upon the surface of the painting, and is only relatively white; similarly the best black pigment fails to absorb all of the light falling on the surface, and is only relatively black. Further inaccuracies and limitations of these scales, especially with regard to hue and intensity intervals, will be discussed later on. For the present, we may confine our attention to our scales and the diagrams connected therewith, in order to obtain a clear understanding of the opportunities which they afford for definite thought and practice in connection with tone relations.

FIG. 1
The Scale
of Values.

The Scale of Values

A convenient scale of values in neutral tones may be produced, as shown in fig. 1 (Plate LXVI), by starting with the limits of *white* (Wt)

[5] Denman W. Ross, *A Theory of Pure Design* (Boston and New York, 1907).

and *black* (Blk), then producing a *middle value* (M) to make the same contrast with both Wt and Blk, further intermediate values of *light* (Lt), halfway between Wt and M, *dark* (D), halfway between M and Blk, and the additional intermediates of *high light* (HLt), *low light* (LLt), *high dark* (HD), and *low dark* (LD).

This scale of nine values gives sufficiently small intervals for ordinary practice and can be easily executed with a surprising degree of accuracy. In water color it may be produced with washes of charcoal gray, or other black pigment, with the paper used for Wt.

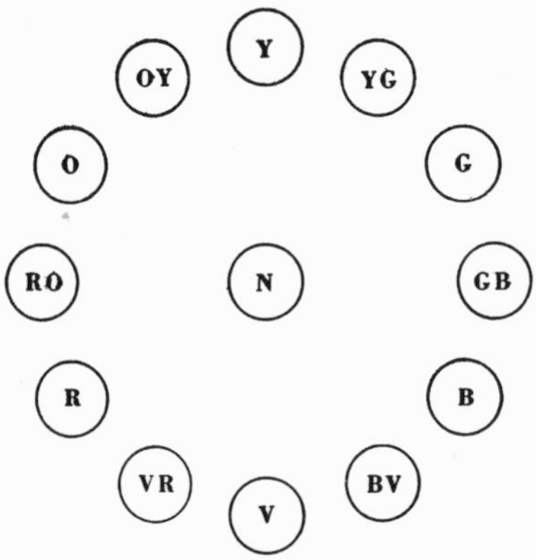

The Scale of Hues

In a similar way we may make a scale of hues, as shown in fig. 2 (Color Chart II), by starting with *red* (R), *yellow* (Y), and *blue* (B), placed at equal intervals in a circular scheme. The hues should all be produced at their highest possible intensities.[6] Intermediates of *orange* (O) to make equal contrast with both R and Y, *green* (G) halfway between Y and B,

FIG. 2. The Scale of Hues.

and *violet* (V) halfway between B and R, and the further intermediates of *red-orange* (RO), *orange-yellow* (OY), *yellow-green* (YG), *green-blue* (GB), *blue-violet* (BV), and *violet-red* (VR), may then be produced. This gives a convenient scale of twelve hues with nearly equal intervals, and approximate pigment complementaries[7]—not true visual complementaries —opposite, so that a line joining a pair of pigment complementaries crosses

[6] For practical purposes the red may be considered as a hue in which there is no suggestion of either orange or violet; the yellow as one which tends neither toward orange nor green; and the blue as tending neither toward green nor violet. These are purely working definitions. It must be borne in mind that this classification of hues is entirely a matter of convenience in working with pigment materials ordinarily used in painting, and that we are not concerned here with the process of color vision.

[7] Complementaries are any two hues which may be mixed in such a way as to produce neutral, or gray. Mixtures of pigments work on the subtractive principle and give different results from those produced by mixtures of light. This is explained in Chapter II.

the center of the circle, where we may place *neutral* or *gray* (N).

This scale may be produced in water color with the following comparatively permanent pigments or mixtures of these: rose madder or alizarin crimson, vermilion, orange cadmium, aureolin or pale cadmium yellow, veridian, cobalt blue, and French ultramarine blue.

It will be noticed that in the hue scale, produced in this way, the different hues at their highest intensities occur at different values. If these are compared with the value scale, it will be found that Y corresponds in value approximately to HLt, that OY and YG come approximately at Lt, O and G at LLt, RO and GB at M, R and B at HD, VR and BV at D, and V at LD. The hues between Y and V on the left of the circle may be spoken of in a general way as *warm* hues, and those on the right as *cold* hues.

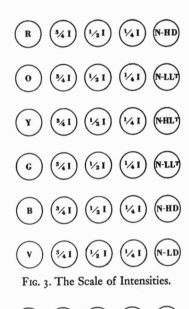

FIG. 3. The Scale of Intensities.

FIG. 4. The Scale of Neutralization.

The Scale of Intensities

A scale of intensities in any hue may be made by starting with the limits of the hue at highest possible intensity and the corresponding neutral of the same value, and then taking intermediates of $\frac{1}{2}$ I, $\frac{1}{4}$ I, and $\frac{3}{4}$ I, as shown for the six main hues in fig. 3 (Color Chart III).

The degree of intensity may be expressed in another way as degree of neutralization, as shown in fig. 4.

The scales of intensities may be produced with the pigments used for the scale of hues with the addition of charcoal gray, but care must be taken to add red and orange respectively in producing the lower intensities of O and Y, in order to overcome the accidental tendency in pigment mixtures for orange to turn toward yellow, and yellow toward green, when these pigments are mixed with a black pigment.

DIAGRAMS OF VALUE AND INTENSITY FOR THE TWELVE HUES

Diagrams expressing graphically the relations of values, hues, and intensities will be found of much assistance in achieving a clear understanding of the principles governing tone relations both in nature and in painting, and especially useful in the consideration of design in tone relations. The value and intensity possibilities of a single hue may be represented as follows.

Let the vertical line in fig. 5 represent the scale of neutral grays from Wt to Blk. Red-orange at its highest intensity comes at the value of M, but it is distinguished from N–M by its hue of red-orange and by the intensity of its hue. If we measure the contrast made by RO at its fullest intensity and N–M, with the contrast made by N–M and higher and lower values of neutral, we shall find that the contrast of RO at highest intensity and N–M about equals in attraction the contrast between N–M and N between Lt and HLt — about two and a half steps of the value scale (fig. 1). We may, then, in the diagram, place RO at its highest intensity at the same level as N–M, and at a distance from N–M laterally as shown in fig. 5 (Color Chart IV). This represents with sufficient accuracy the value and intensity of RO at its greatest intensity in relation to Wt and Blk and neutrals between them.

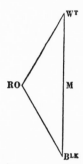

FIG. 5. The Value and Intensity Possibilities of Red-Orange.

In order to raise the value of RO above M we must introduce the element of white or of some other neutral above M. If we introduce the element of white, we carry the RO toward Wt along the line from RO to Wt. In order to lower the value of RO we must introduce the element of Blk or of some other neutral below M. If we introduce the element of Blk, we move RO along the line RO to Blk. The triangle RO–Wt–Blk expresses the possibilities of the hue of red-orange. We may have the hue quality of red-orange at any of the values and intensities within the limits of this triangle.

We may make similar diagrams for each of the twelve hues of the hue scale, as shown in fig. 6. For the sake of simplicity in the diagrams, it is arbitrarily assumed that the different hues at their greatest intensity

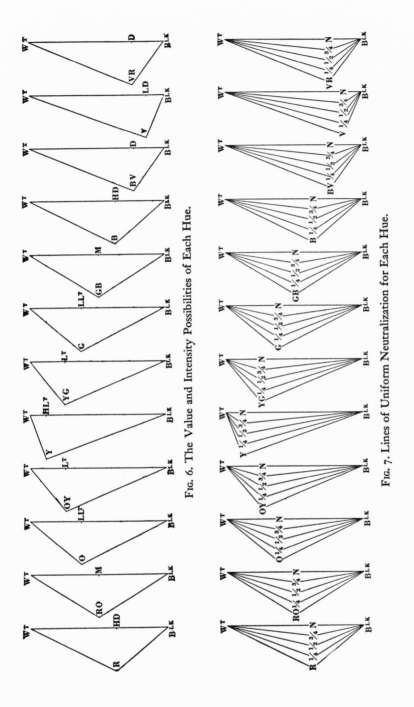

Fig. 6. The Value and Intensity Possibilities of Each Hue.

Fig. 7. Lines of Uniform Neutralization for Each Hue.

are of equal intensity. The triangles are thus all made the same width.[8]

On each of the vertical lines in the RO triangle shown in fig. 8 there is *uniformity of intensity*. There is *uniformity of value* on each of the horizontal lines.

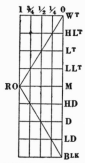

FIG. 8. Triangle of RO with Lines of Uniform Value and Uniform Intensity.

FIG. 9. Triangle of RO with Lines of Uniform Neutralization.

In fig. 9 the inclined lines from RO to Wt, and from RO to Blk, represent the highest intensities of RO which can be obtained at the different value levels.[9] The other inclined lines indicate different degrees of neutralization from the highest intensities at the different value levels.

The neutralization lines in each of the twelve triangles are shown in fig. 7.

A tone may be defined either in regard to its intensity — its distance from the neutral line — or it may be defined with regard to its degree of neutralization from the highest intensity of the hue obtainable at the particular value. Thus:

RO–M–$\frac{1}{4}$ I is the same as RO–M–$\frac{3}{4}$ N (neutralized).

[8] To be perfectly accurate the triangles should be drawn with different widths. Investigations should be carried out to determine the exact shapes of the different triangles, and, as nearly as possible, the shape of the true tone solid which would express the complete possibilities of value, hue, and intensity for a given white light. We do not know definitely that the outer sides of the hue triangles should not be curved rather than straight lines. Troland in an earlier report of the Colorimetry Committee of the Optical Society (Leonard T. Troland, Chairman; Journal of the Optical Society of America, August, 1922, p. 546), even suggests a doubt as to whether the space of the tone solid is Euclidean.

[9] These lines have no significance except as a means of convenient notation.

RO–Lt–$\frac{1}{2}$ I is the same as RO–Lt (the highest intensity of RO obtainable at that value).

RO–D–$\frac{1}{4}$ I is the same as RO–D–$\frac{1}{2}$ N.

In most cases it is more convenient to define tones by their degree of neutralization, as in the second alternative shown in each case above. Thus: R–HD; R–HLt (the highest intensity of R at that value); R–M–$\frac{3}{4}$ N; O–D–$\frac{1}{4}$ N; G–Lt; G–HD–$\frac{1}{2}$ N; and so forth.[10]

THE WORKING TONE SOLID

A three-dimensional diagram, expressing relations of values, hues, and intensities, may be made by taking the triangles of the twelve hues and placing them so that their neutral lines coincide, forming a vertical axis from which the triangles radiate in the order of the hue circle (fig. 2). The side elevation of this three-dimensional diagram or tone solid may be constructed as shown in fig. 10.

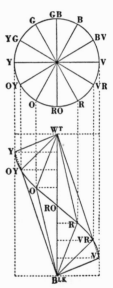

FIG. 10. The Working Tone Solid Derived from the Hue Triangles.

A wooden model of this tone solid may be easily carved out of a cylindrical piece of wood. The hues at their fullest intensities all touch the surface of the cylinder.

This tone solid, constructed on the basis of the twelve triangles, is arbitrarily symmetrical; but it will be found very helpful as a means of getting an understanding of the main facts in connection with tone relations. The neutral line from Wt to Blk forms the axis of the solid. As we move up or down, we get changes of value; as we moved outward or inward in relation to the vertical axis, we get changes of intensity; as we move around the axis, we get changes of hue. At each horizontal level there is uniform value; on each radiating vertical plane, there is uniform hue; on the surface of any of a series of concentric cylinders, there is approximately uniform intensity.

A chart of the twelve hues in their highest intensities at each of the

[10] Intermediate hues between any of the twelve hues in this classification might be defined as plus or minus a given hue, reading the circle clockwise. Intermediate values and intensities may be distinguished in a similar manner.

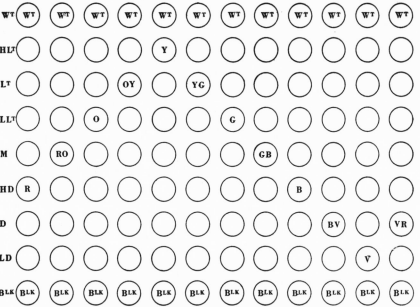

Fɪɢ. 11. Diagram of the Chart Showing the Highest Possible Intensities of the
Twelve Hues at Seven Different Value Levels between White and Black.

seven values between Wt and Blk, as shown in fig. 11 (Color Chart V),
gives all the main tones on the outside surface of the tone solid.

This chart may be produced in water color with the same pigments
as the scales of hues and of intensities (figs. 2 and 3) with the addition
of burnt sienna to be used in making the lower values of O, OY, and Y.
As in the scale of intensities, care must be taken to correct the tendency
in pigments for the mixture of yellow and orange with black to swing
toward green.

In this chart vertical rows are uniform in hue, and horizontal rows
are uniform in value. In connection with the horizontal sections of the
tone solid, as shown in fig. 12, this chart, when carefully made, shows
clearly the possibilities of hue and intensity at the different value levels.
At the value of HLt, Y comes at highest intensity, while OY and YG
can be obtained only at considerably less intensity, O and G at still
lower intensity, and the violet region, V, VR, and BV, only at very
low intensities. The linear distances between the various tones in the
diagram, fig. 12, express the relative strength of the contrasts between the
corresponding tones in fig. 11 (Color Chart V). At the value of Lt, OY

15

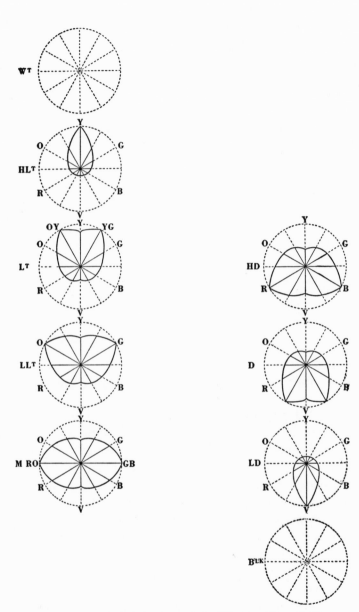

Fig. 12. Horizontal Sections of the Working Tone Solid
at the Principal Different Value Levels.

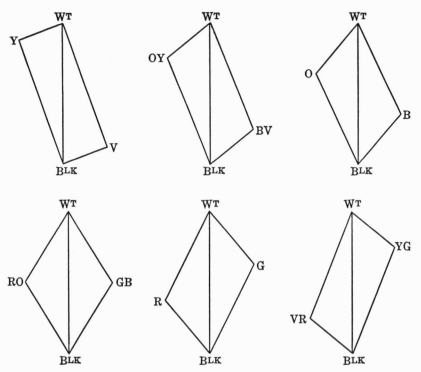

FIG. 13. The Principal Vertical Sections of the Working Tone Solid.

and YG reach highest intensity, while Y moves in toward the neutral center, and the violets and the other hues become a little more intense and, in the diagram, move out farther toward the outside of the circle. At M, RO and GB are at highest intensity, while violets and yellows are comparatively middling in intensity. Finally, at LD, the yellow region shows low intensities and limited contrasts, while violet reaches its highest intensity. The yellows and oranges in the lower values are what are in ordinary speech vaguely called browns, red-browns or olive-browns; but the distinctions in hue quality, though less in degree, are exactly the same as in the higher values. It must be borne in mind that any hue may be obtained at any value between Wt and Blk.

Vertical sections of the tone solid, as in fig. 13, show the hue triangles in pairs of complementary hues.

THE DIAGRAM OF HUES AND INTENSITIES

While it is necessary to use the three-dimensional diagram of the tone solid to express relations of values, hues, and intensities, all at the same time, and to represent complete contrasts between tones accurately, two-dimensional diagrams may be used to express relations of any two factors without regard to the third, and are very useful in actual practice.

By means of the circular plan of the tone solid, fig. 14, we may express relations of hue and intensity without regard to value. This is very useful, for instance, as a basis for thinking of mixtures of pigments ordinarily used in painting, as shown in fig. 15.

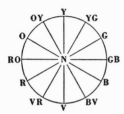

Fig. 14. Diagram of Hues and Intensities — the Plan of the Tone Solid.

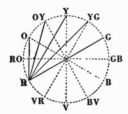

Fig. 15. Diagram of Hues and Intensities, Showing Results of Mixing Pigments.

If a red pigment is mixed with orange, the mixture falls approximately along the line R–O — there is slight loss of the intensity of the two hues. If the R is mixed with OY, the mixture falls along the line R–OY. The halfway point is between O and RO, slightly nearer the neutral center. If the R is mixed with Y, the mixture falls along the line R–Y, and the halfway point is on the O radius, still nearer the N center. If the R is mixed with YG, the halfway point, between the O and OY radii, is very close to the N center. Finally, if the R is mixed with G, the halfway point is N, and the other possibilities are various intensities of R and G, along the line R–N–G.

Although, as explained in the next chapter, the results of pigment mixing are not perfectly certain unless one knows the part of the light that is absorbed and the part reflected by each one, almost all ordinary pigment mixtures may be thought out on the basis of this diagram, so far as hue and intensity possibilities are concerned. If, for example, we are painting a landscape with burnt sienna, yellow ochre, and cobalt blue, the limits of hue and intensity to be obtained by this combination are explained in the diagram, fig. 16. If a portrait is painted in R, Y, and N (red, yellow, and white and black pigments), as in so many portraits by the later Renaissance masters, the diagram, fig. 17, explains

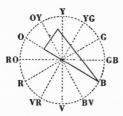

Fig. 16. Approximate Limitations of Hue and Intensity Involved in the Use of Burnt Sienna, Yellow Ochre, and Cobalt Blue.

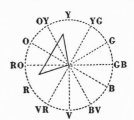

Fig. 17. Approximate Limitations of Hue and Intensity Involved in Much Venetian Painting.

the limits of hue and intensity to be obtained by this combination. In this case what counts as neutral in the painting is usually a low intensity of OY, and the N tells in the painting as relative blue.

THE DIAGRAM OF VALUES AND INTENSITIES

A vertical diagram to express relations of value and intensity may be made by conceiving the different hue triangles to be turned into the same plane around the neutral axis, and arranged right and left of

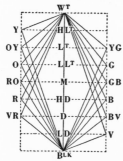

Fig. 18. Diagram of Values and Intensities.

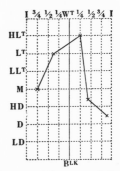

Fig. 19. Diagram of Values and Intensities with an Indication of Relative Contrasts.

this axis, as shown in fig. 18. Individual tones may be plotted at different levels to show value, and at different distances right and left of the neutral line to show intensity, as in fig. 19. Lines joining these tones in the diagram indicate the approximate contrasts between the different tones. This diagram is useful in many ways. For example, it helps to explain the general principle governing the changes of tone as objects model from light to dark in nature, as explained in Chapter 4 and shown in fig. 33. By a similar diagram the actual practice of most of the medieval and earlier Renaissance masters may also be shown (as in figs. 41 and 42 in Chapter 6).

THE DIAGRAM OF VALUES AND HUES

A diagram expressing relations of values and hues, without regard to intensity, consists of the various triangles of the tone solid projected upon the surface of the enclosing cylinder, and unfolded on a flat plane,

Wт	.	.	.	.	.	.	.	.	.	.	.	.
HLт	.	.	.	Y	.	.	.	.	.	.		
Lт	.	.	. OY	.	YG	.	.	.	.	.		
LLт	.	. O	.	.	.	. G	.	.	.	.		
M	. RO	.	.	.	. GB	.	.	.	.		
HD	R	.	.	.	.	.	. B	.	.	.		
D	.	.	.	.	.	.	. BV	. VR			
LD	.	.	.	.	.	.	. V	.			
Blk	.	.	.	.	.	.	.	.	.	.		

FIG. 20. Diagram of Values and Hues.

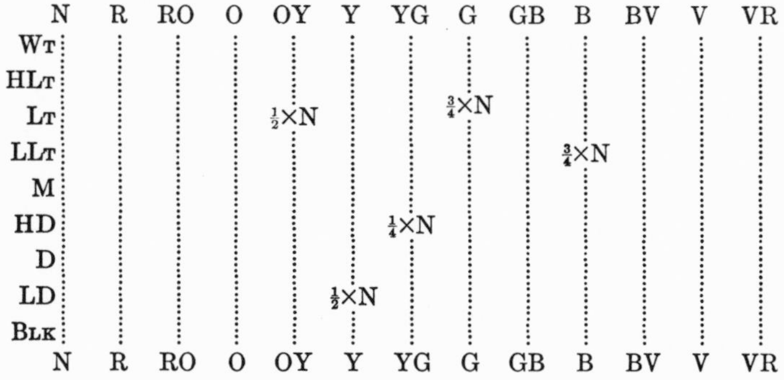

FIG. 21. Diagram of Values and Hues with Plotting of Specific Tones.

as in fig. 20. In this figure the triangles are each represented by a vertical line, as if seen edge on. This diagram will be found especially useful in plotting tones from the standpoint of design. By indicating the degree of neutralization with figures, as in fig. 21, a complete score of a composition may be recorded. This diagram corresponds to the chart shown in fig. 11.

The classification described above gives a useful terminology and the working tone solid provides a three-dimensional diagram and a convenient series of two-dimensional diagrams by means of which relationships of different tones may be expressed. The limitations of this solid and its relation to other tone or color solids which have been devised will be considered in the next chapter.

2

QUALIFICATIONS AND LIMITATIONS OF THE WORKING TONE SOLID · OTHER TONE SOLIDS · A TRUE TONE SOLID · PURITY AND BRILLIANCE

ADDITIVE AND SUBTRACTIVE MIXING

The impossibility of producing perfect tone scales in pigment materials was referred to in the last chapter. It was also stated that the scales and diagrams there set forth were made deliberately more or less inaccurate for the sake of the convenience of the painter. In this one is perhaps somewhat justified by the analogy of the tempered scale of the pianoforte, which is likewise conveniently inaccurate; only our scales are rather more violently tempered.

The principal difficulty in the way of making a tone solid which shall combine convenience for the painter with scientific accuracy, lies in the fact that the mixture of pigments of different hues gives results frequently quite different from those obtained by the mixture of light of these same hues. Thus, when we mix yellow and blue pigments, the result is ordinarily a greenish tone; and when we mix yellow and violet pigments, the result is a neutral. On the other hand, when we mix a yellow stream of light and a violet stream of light, the result is a reddish or orange tone; and when we mix yellow light and blue light, the result is neutral instead of green. This is due to the fact that there are two different methods of mixing tones. These are known as the additive and subtractive methods respectively, and they may be explained as follows.

Suppose that we have two lanterns throwing streams of white light on the screen at C, in fig. 23, and suppose that we place a yellow screen in lantern A and a blue screen in lantern B. We may also suppose, for the sake of simplicity, that white or neutral light is composed of a mixture of R, O, Y, G, B, and V rays. The particular hue of light reflected by a pigment is of course due to the fact that the pigment material has the power of absorbing certain of the wave lengths of white light and of reflecting or transmitting others. The particular hue is that of the dominant wave length among those reflected; but in addition to the dominant wave length adjacent wave lengths covering a considerable portion of the spectrum are ordinarily reflected. The "spread" over the spectrum of some of the common pigment materials is shown in the diagram of relative wave lengths and energy from Luckiesh given in fig. 22.[1]

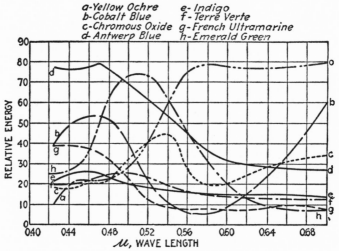

FIG. 22. Spectral Analyses of Pigments.

Let us suppose that the yellow pigment in the screen of lantern A in fig. 23 has the power of absorbing the B and V rays out of the white light, and of transmitting the rest, namely the R, O, Y, and G, among which the Y is dominant; and that the blue pigment, on the other hand, absorbs the R, O, and Y, and transmits the G, B, and V, among which the blue is dominant. If we add the two streams together, we have all the component elements of white light in the resulting mixture, and the mixture is neutral, as shown in fig. 23.

On the other hand, if we shut off lantern B and put both the Y and the B screens in lantern A, part of the rays of white light are absorbed by the Y, and still more by the B, leaving only the G transmitted to

[1] M. Luckiesh, *Color and its Application* (New York, 1915), fig. 122, p. 298.

the screen, as shown in fig. 24. If we should put in also a red screen, this would absorb the G rays, and no light of any kind would be transmitted to the screen at C. In other words the result of the mixture would be black.[2]

These are of course only approximate diagrams. In fig. 25 the possible mixture of Y and a visual complementary B is indicated in a diagram in which relative wave lengths (μ) are shown horizontally and relative energy vertically.[3] This shows the "spread" of the light reflected by each pigment material over the spectrum. Practically all

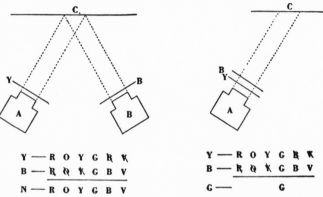

FIG. 23. Additive Mixing of Hue.   FIG. 24. Subtractive Mixing of Hue.

pigment materials reflect a considerable range of wave lengths in addition to the dominant wave length which gives the particular hue, as is shown in fig. 22.

Pigments mix approximately on the subtractive principle. Finely divided particles of different colors are so intermingled that light travels perhaps first through a yellow particle and then through a blue particle, even several times over, before being reflected back from the

[2] The results obtained by subtractive mixing depend on the spectral distribution of the light transmitted by the pigments or dyes involved. There are actually yellow and blue pigments or dyes which in subtractive mixture give red. Without knowledge of the spectral distribution the visual result is unpredictable. Nevertheless, as pointed out earlier, for ordinary pigments used in painting, the resulting tone usually falls approximately on the straight line in the hue circle joining the two original tones. If the mixture falls on a slightly curved instead of a straight line, allowance can be made visually.

[3] The order of hues and wave lengths, as usually shown in physics, is reversed. Cf. fig. 22.

surface of the painting. This accounts for the fact that there is always some lowering of value when pigments are mixed together, though at times it is so slight as to make no appreciable difference. The stronger the intensities and the greater the hue interval, the greater will be the lowering of value in the mixture. It is partly for this reason that it is wise to avoid too intimate a mixing of the tones on the palette in actual painting.[4]

In the "color-top," or the Clerk–Maxwell discs, on the other hand, the mixture conforms to the additive principle. Owing to the phenomenon known as persistence of vision, the alternating streams of Y and B falling on the retina of the eye produce much the same effect as in the case of the streams from the two lanterns in fig. 23.

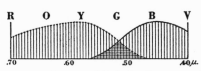

FIG. 25. Diagram of Relative Energy and Relative Wave Length.

Continuous line indicates reflecting power of a possbile B pigment for all wave lengths (μ). Dotted line indicates reflecting power of a possible Y pigment for all wave lengths. Result of additive method is shown by vertical shading. Result of subtractive method is shown by horizontal shading.

When the tones in a painting are juxtaposed in the "pointillist" or "divisionist" fashion, instead of being mixed on the palette or on the brush in the ordinary way, there is a more or less close approach to mixture of streams of light on the additive principle, as in rotation, when the picture is looked at from a considerable distance.[5] It is seldom that a painting can be satisfactorily handled completely in this manner, but there is often some compromise between mixture by addition and mixture by subtraction.[6]

[4] See Luckiesh, *op. cit.*, pp. 297–301, and figs. 122–124.
[5] Lumière color photography is based on this principle.
[6] In painting one does not ordinarily have to pay much attention to the matter of additive mixing, for, except for a slight amount of additive mixing in the use of broken color, or possibly a good deal in the unusual use of an extreme method of "pointillism," pigment mixtures work on the subtractive basis; but in all work on the stage one is dealing constantly with additive as well as subtractive mixing. When, for example, light of different hues from two or more light sources is thrown on a plaster dome or a cyclorama, the overlapping of the streams of light of different hues results in an additive mixing. There is a certain amount of additive mixing whenever streams of light from different sources overlap on any of the objects on the stage. But there is also usually a good deal of subtractive mixing mingled with this. The pigments or dyes used in the gelatine screens which are placed in the various light sources are all subtractive agents; so are all the

Munsell [7] worked out a hue scale on the principle of rotation. This consists of five hues taken at equal intervals, as in fig. 26. When equal areas of these five hues at the same value and at the same intensity are rotated, as in the Munsell sphere, they produce neutral. They are at equal intervals for mixture on the additive principle.

In the tone solid shown in the last chapter the intervals between the hues correspond approximately to ordinary pigment mixtures; ap-

 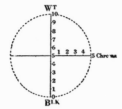 

FIG. 26. Scale of Five Hues, Based on Additive Mixing, like that of Munsell.

FIG. 27. Diagrams Illustrating Partial Inaccuracy of Munsell Color Sphere.

proximate pigment complementaries — not true complementaries — are placed in opposing pairs.

FURTHER LIMITATIONS OF THE WORKING TONE SOLID

A marked defect in the tone solid shown in the last chapter lies in the fact that the triangles of the twelve hues are made all the same width, although the hues produced at the highest intensities obtainable with our pigment materials are not all of the same intensity. The RO of our hue scale is much more intense than the GB, for example. In

pigment materials used in painting the scenery and dyeing the costumes. So when a colored light falls on a costume other than white, the resulting tone is a matter of subtractive mixing — a part of the white light is absorbed by the screen and still more by the pigment material in the costume. For instance, the usual amber screen used in stage lighting absorbs all the blue region of the spectrum; so when amber light is thrown on a blue dress the latter looks gray or black — it cannot reflect any blue unless there is some blue in the light coming to it, and there is no blue in this case. The changes in value as well as hue and intensity are sometimes very startling, as the tone of the light is changed; often they are quite inexplicable to the person who knows nothing of color theory. The lighting man on the stage must know something of the spectral composition of the dyes in his gelatine screens, and also of the pigments used in the painting of the scenery and the dyes used in the costumes, before he can tell even approximately what effect his lights are going to produce.

[7] *Op. cit.*

order to make a tone solid which would express intensity relations
accurately, it would be necessary to vary the width of the triangles
according to the relative contrasts of intensities and values. This would
produce an irregular instead of a symmetrical solid.

This difficulty is avoided in Munsell's sphere by placing what he
calls No. 5 chromas (exactly uniform intensities) on the equator of
the sphere, all the same distance from the neutral axis. There is an error
in this, however, in that the relation between intensity (or chroma)
contrasts and value contrasts is not observed. Consequently in Munsell's
diagrams showing the highest intensities (chromas) of the different
hues, these are placed at great distances from the neutral axis, indicating, for instance, a contrast between R at its highest intensity and N of
the same value greater than the contrast between Wt and Blk. As a
matter of fact, the latter contrast is much greater, and the Munsell
sphere and other solids and diagrams are not thoroughly accurate in
this respect. The sphere, to be perfectly accurate, ought to be a bobbin-
shaped figure of smaller diameter, approximately as indicated in fig. 27.[8]

A fact to be noted in connection with the Munsell charts is that
they are based on tones produced with opaque pigments, and higher
intensities may usually be produced in transparent or semitransparent
pigments than in opaque pigments. The highest intensities come at
different value levels when produced with transparent pigments. On
the other hand, they do not correspond exactly to the values of the
value scale, as would be indicated by the symmetrical tone solid. The
highest intensity of V, for example, comes considerably above LD,
though possibly the greatest purity of V may be obtained at about that
value (see farther on in this chapter), and G is probably placed at
somewhat too high a value. This is a further inaccuracy of the symmetrical tone solid; nevertheless in a general way the steady descent of the
high intensity line from Y to V, through either the warm or the cold
hues, would probably be a feature of the true tone solid.

In spite of the limitations noted above, the symmetrical tone solid
and the scales derived from it are convenient devices to be used as aids

[8] In the *Munsell Book of Color*, the charts of values and chromas (intensities)
for single hues are reduced in width by the omission of alternate chromas and
also by making the separate patches rectangular; the shapes of the charts thus
correspond more closely to those of our triangles of value and intensity.

to definite thinking about tone relations, and it may be noticed that in painting we are interested in relations rather than in mere specifications. The scales are easily produced, and even memorized, with approximate accuracy, so that a painter, indeed anyone, may very quickly make use of them and the various diagrams connected with them almost unconsciously.

The advantage of this solid over other solids so far devised is that lines drawn from point to point in the solid represent with approximate accuracy the contrasts made by the corresponding tones when juxtaposed on a flat surface. This is not true, for instance, of the Ostwald solid,[9] in which the "full colors" (high intensities) are placed at the same level without regard to their differences in value so that distances from point to point in the solid have no meaning; nor is it true of the Munsell solid, although the latter may be adjusted to give more nearly accurate relationships for additive mixing and may be used for special purposes. In a similar way, if a thoroughly accurate solid for additive mixing could be worked out it also could be used for purposes requiring greater accuracy in measuring true visual relations; but this would not do away with the advantage of the working solid for many other purposes where allowance for slight inaccuracies can easily be made, and especially when the main consideration is what happens to mixtures of paint. At present, when it is desirable for certain problems, the charts in the *Munsell Book of Color* [10] may be used for reference, although certain inaccuracies in these, especially in the matter of intensities (or chromas), must be corrected by eye.[11]

THE DISTINCT FACTORS OF PURITY AND BRILLIANCE

One difficulty that has constantly produced confusion of thought as well as of terminology in connection with the general consideration of tone or color has been the constant failure on the part of both physicists and psychologists to distinguish between the factor which I have called

[9] Wilhelm Ostwald, *Colour Science*, translation by J. Scott Taylor (London, 1931).

[10] *Op. cit.*

[11] Morton C. Bradley, Jr., "Systems of Color Classification," *Technical Studies in the Field of the Fine Arts*, Fogg Museum of Art, Harvard University, Cambridge, Mass., Vol. VI, No. 4 (April, 1938).

intensity — and is by Munsell called chroma — and a different factor which is usually called purity or saturation; and to distinguish also between what I have here called value and a different factor which is sometimes called brightness, but may be conveniently called brilliance.

In order to define any tone accurately from the visual or psychological point of view, it is only necessary to state its hue and value and intensity (chroma); but the two further factors, which I shall call *purity* and *brilliance*, must be considered if one is to possess a complete understanding of the subject. As a matter of fact a tone could be defined by stating its hue, brilliance, and purity, instead of its hue, value, and intensity, and this method of classification has been sometimes used.[12] It is necessary to distinguish clearly between these two systems of classification and the factors involved in each of them, for this is not, as has often been supposed, merely a matter of the use of equivalent terms for the same factors.

Let us suppose that we have a pigment which when spread over a flat surface gives us the hue of orange; that this pigment is, for the sake of simplification of argument, of such a quality that it reflects perfectly all orange wave lengths out of white light which falls upon the painted surface, but that it absorbs all of the other wave lengths. We have then orange of absolute purity, and also of highest possible energy. In a diagram of values and intensities, as in fig. 28, in which the white and black are assumed to be perfect white and perfect black, the orange sensation produced by this perfect orange pigment, being of highest possible intensity or chroma for this particular hue, will come, let us suppose, at O. If the strength of the illumination on the painting surface is lowered until the white is lowered to Wt′, the orange will be reduced to O′. If the illumination is lowered still farther until white comes at Wt″, the orange will fall to O″ in fig. 28. It is possible that these changes in tone might also be achieved by changes in the quality of the pigment — that is, if we could add a perfect black pigment to the orange. If we call the common visual quality in the different tones along the line O–Blk in fig. 28 *purity*, we may say that all the tones along the line O–Blk are of uniform purity, and of uniform maximum purity.

---

[12] This method has apparently been used by Ruxton. See L. C. Martin and W. Gamble, *Colour and Methods of Colour Reproduction* (New York, 1923), p. 30, and Luckiesh, *op. cit.*, pp. 82–84.

White added to the orange would diminish its purity along the line
O–Wt. If a scale of relative purity were measured along this line, the
diagonal lines between the line O–Blk and the line Wt–Blk would be
lines of uniform relative purity, as shown in fig. 28.

The orange pigment assumed in the above is supposed to reflect the
orange wave length at its full strength or energy. As the orange is

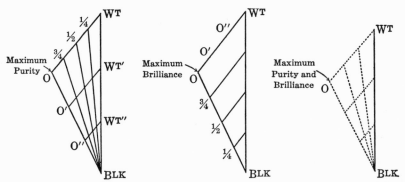

FIG. 28. Diagram of Value and Intensity Possibilities of Orange, Showing Lines of Uniform Relative Purity.

FIG. 29. Lines of Uniform Relative Brilliance of Orange.

FIG. 30. Relative Values and Intensities of Tones in a Classification Based on Purity and Brilliance.

carried along the line O–Wt, more and more of the energy of the other
wave lengths of white light is added to the orange, but the full strength
or energy of the orange wave length remains as a component element
in the tones all the way to white. If we call the common visual quality
in the different tones along the line O–Wt, due to the presence of the
full energy of the orange wave length in all these tones, *brilliance*, we
may say that all the tones along the line O–Wt are of uniform brilliance,
and of uniform maximum brilliance. If a scale of relative brilliance is
measured along the line O–Blk, lines drawn from the various points of
this scale to the neutral line Wt–Blk parallel to the line O–Wt will be
lines of uniform relative brilliance, like the lines O′–Wt′ and O″–Wt″
in fig. 28, or the lines of $\frac{1}{4}$, $\frac{1}{2}$, and $\frac{3}{4}$ brilliance in fig. 29.

Now, let us turn for a moment to the treatment of the matter in
one or two scientific books. In *Color and Its Application* by Luckiesh,[13]
on page 80, the term saturation is used as the equivalent of Munsell's

[13] *Op. cit.*

chroma and our term intensity; but on page 71 it is used in the entirely different sense of purity as I have defined it above. Luckiesh writes:

On diluting a color with white light, tints are obtained; that is, tints are unsaturated colors. By the admixture of black to a color (in effect the same as reducing the intensity of illumination) the brightness is diminished without altering either the hue or the saturation, and various shades are produced.

The "tints," in our diagram in fig. 28, would come on the line O–Wt, and the "shades," obtained by the "admixture of black . . . without altering . . . the saturation," would come on the line O–Blk; and on this line there is steady "alteration" of chroma or intensity all the way to Blk. This is, I believe, a perfectly proper sense in which to use the term saturation; but if it is used in this sense, it must not be supposed that it is equivalent to chroma or intensity.[14]

To take another example, in *Colour and Methods of Colour Reproduction* by Martin and Gamble,[15] on page 12, saturation, purity, and chroma are grouped together as equivalent terms; but on page 30 is the following passage referring to the Ruxton classification of tones or colors:

Each spectral hue is shown in three saturations [the two weaker saturations are described in this case as being made by mixing white with the pigment at highest saturation], and each saturation is shown in three degrees of brightness (the diminution of "value" being secured by the addition of black).

In the case of orange the tones obtained by this arrangement would be placed on the diagram of values and intensities as shown in fig. 30.

Here both the terms brightness and saturation are used in the sense of brilliance and purity as I have defined them above. They are also used in this same sense in the following passage from Martin and Gamble:

Having formed the conception of a pure hue (which may or may not be found quite ideally in the spectrum), we may now conceive a

[14] It is to avoid confusion, since the Colorimetry Committee of The Optical Society uses the term saturation as equivalent to our intensity, that I am herein proposing the use of the term *purity* to distinguish this factor.
[15] *Op. cit.*

wide range of perceptibly differing colours formed from it, for we might proceed to dilute the hue with differing amounts of white (keeping the total light always to a standard intensity) and thus form a tint series or series of differing saturation. Further, with any number of the same series the "brightness" may be varied from zero upwards in a great number of perceptible steps until a "dazzling" brightness is reached. This produces a series of shades of a pure hue.[16]

In another passage on the same page brightness is defined as follows:

The brightness of coloured light may be assumed to consist generally of two parts: (1) the brightness of the component which also causes the pure sensation of hue, and (2) the brightness of any white sensation which may be present.

Just before this sentence is the following:

The saturation, purity, or chroma of a colour refers to the proportion of the brightness of the pure hue sensation to the total brightness of the colour.

Chroma is here used as equivalent to purity, and no allowance is made for the use of chroma in the sense in which it is defined by Munsell or for any other word to indicate what we have spoken of as intensity, which is the exact equivalent of Munsell's chroma.

Titchener[17] on the other hand uses saturation as the equivalent of chroma according to the Munsell definition. The Report of the Colorimetry Committee of the Optical Society of America defines saturation in the same way, while, like Titchener, it fails to distinguish the factor called here purity.

The difficulty is that Martin and Gamble, along with Luckiesh and other scientific authorities, have failed to see that purity and brilliance, as defined above, are distinct from the factors of value and chroma or intensity. As shown in the accompanying diagrams, the lines of uniform relative purity and brilliance cut diagonally across the lines representing uniformity of value and of chroma or intensity, which are horizontal and vertical, respectively.

[16] *Op. cit.*, p. 12.
[17] E. B. Titchener, *A Textbook of Psychology* (New York, 1928).

As a matter of fact the term saturation is, I believe, the more appropriate term to be used for the factor which I define here as purity, and, as shown in the passages quoted above, it has very naturally, if often unconsciously, been used in this sense. However the use of saturation as the equivalent of intensity or chroma has become so common among scientific writers that a resort to the less satisfactory term of purity has under the circumstances seemed unavoidable. The matter of the choice of terms is at any rate largely academic. Nevertheless, purity (or saturation in this sense) has definite visual and design significance, and so also has brilliance. There is a uniformity of quality in the tones along the line O–Blk which can be appreciated visually even when this is only approximated by pigment mixtures. It is a principal factor, as is shown later on, in giving an orderly relationship to the tones we observe every day as objects about us pass from light into shadow. There is a similar uniformity of quality in the tones along the line O–Wt, and this is also appreciable in the approximations of pigment mixtures. In other words, there is a uniformity of brillance in all the tones on the upper surface of the tone solid. This is illustrated roughly in Plate LXX, where all the upper tones in each vertical row are obtained by mixing the full intensity of each hue with white. These tones are what are sometimes referred to as *tints*,[18] as in the passage quoted from Luckiesh. In much of the painting of the so-called Impressionists, like Monet, Renoir, and Dodge MacKnight, the tones employed are confined to the upper surface of the tone solid. Thus there is in their works a harmony of highest possible brilliance; each color, being either at highest possible intensity or else mixed only with white, is maintained, as nearly as is possible in pigment materials, at the strength of illumination which it possesses as a component of the white light falling on the surface of the painting. As a hypothesis which seems to work in actual practice, I believe that this accounts principally for the feeling of brilliant and harmonious light in the works of these painters. As explained in the discussion of the use of limited palettes in a later chapter, the transposition into the Monet or MacKnight palette is a perfectly arbitrary artistic device, and not a matter of mere breaking up of white

[18] The extended use of classifications which discriminate between *tints* and *shades* is, I believe, an indication of the fact that there are common qualities in uniform brilliances and uniform purities (or saturations) which are visually appreciable.

light into its spectral components, according to the explanation frequently given.

All this discussion seems unnecessarily technical and complicated for a book on the art of painting; but where there is so much confusion of thought, it seems sensible, if it is possible, to clarify our ideas. I think it is not improbable that the treatment of purity and brilliance as separate factors, distinct from value and intensity, may throw some further light on the very complex subject of design in tone relations. This is dealt with briefly in the section on design in tone relations in the Appendix; but so far there has not been enough experimentation to determine whether the possibility has any great significance or not.[19]

Curiously enough in the Ostwald solid,[20] in which the "full colors" are all placed on the equator opposite middle value, in spite of their actual value differences, and the triangles are made arbitrarily equilateral, each of the vertical lines parallel to the neutral axis represents what Ostwald calls a "shadow series" — a line of uniform purity according to our definition of this term. The purity in this case is absolute, representing a descent in value and intensity toward absolute black. A black is assumed, though this is not clearly explained, below the black of black paint and is thus represented by a horizontal line or, in the solid, a plane extending to the lateral limits of the solid. Theoretically, and in some cases practically, each of the vertical lines may be extended beyond the line from full intensity to black paint down toward this line or plane of absolute black.

Harmony is assumed by Ostwald to exist between tones similarly placed in the solid with relation to white and black. If, as is assumed by Ostwald and his followers, there is, for instance, a uniformity of quality in all tones carried the same degree from full intensity to white, regardless of their value differences, which can be felt as a definite harmony, the solid may have significance from this point of view; but this is still rather problematical. The harmony felt may be due rather

[19] Bradley in *Systems of Color Classification* (*op. cit.*) makes purity (saturation) an absolute, according to the formula: chroma = value $\times$ purity (saturation), regardless of hue; or: purity (saturation) = $\dfrac{\text{chroma}}{\text{value}}$. According to this red at high intensity at value HD would have a greater purity (saturation) than yellow at high intensity at value HLT. I must confess some scepticism in regard to this assumption.

[20] *Op. cit.*

to an approximate uniformity of value of a kind suggested in a later chapter. As I have pointed out elsewhere,[21] exact intervals and exact uniformities have not the same significance in vision that they have in sound; otherwise a slight change in the tone of the light falling on a surface would so affect the exact relations that discords would result as would happen in the case of sound, and this is obviously not true. A textile pattern which looks well in a slightly cool light will probably look well in a slightly warmer light; but the intervals may be very different.

As pointed out before, in the Ostwald solid the distances from point to point have no significance in the representation of relative contrasts. Moreover, the steps between the tones selected are not even, since the actual distance from yellow to white is much less than that from blue or violet to white. On the other hand, from the point of view of mere specification or matching, the recently published *Color Harmony Manual*[22] based on the Ostwald classification, with its movable tabs representing the different tones, may in some cases be very useful.

In the charts of the *Munsell Book of Color*,[23] as Bradley[24] has pointed out, the vertical rows in each triangle are supposed to be of uniform chroma or intensity, but, as actually produced, represent a compromise between chroma (or intensity) and purity.

This is simply further evidence of the fact that, even among scientifically trained persons, confusion of thought in regard to the general problem of tone or color has not even yet entirely disappeared. It testifies also to the recentness of any attempt to think definitely about the subject.

[21] "Notes on the Problem of Color Harmony and the Geometry of Color Space," Journal of the Optical Society of America, Vol. 34, No. 12 (December, 1944).

[22] Egbert Jacobson, *The Color Harmony Manual* (Chicago: Container Corporation of America, 1942).

[23] *Op. cit.*

[24] *Op. cit.*

PART TWO

MODES OF REPRESENTATION IN DRAWING AND PAINTING

3

THE VISUAL IMAGE AND VISUAL CONCEPTS

In the art of painting we make use of an arrangement of tones, produced with pigments spread over a flat surface, to express certain ideas; and, except in the case of purely abstract design, these ideas depend primarily on the representation of natural objects, of natural scenes, or of things imagined as they might appear if they did exist.[1] In much modern painting, as in the mechanical painting or drawing produced by the camera in the form of the photograph, this has to do with the complete literal appearance of things — in other words with the complete visual effect as it is projected in camera-like fashion upon the retina of the eye. But in a large part of painting, and much of this among the finest that has been produced, there has been no thought of representing the complete appearance of things in literal fashion. In fact, drawing or painting is often a rendering of mental concepts which have, to be sure, been formed by means of visual experience but which are nevertheless far from being an exact recording of that experience. In other words our concept of an object formed on the basis of an interpretation of the projection on the retina of the eye is very seldom identical with that projection or image, and we may express our concept of the object in the terms of drawing or painting without in any way imitating its exact image.

For instance we look at a cubical box and we say that we *see* it as an object with three sets of parallel sides, without being at all conscious of the peculiar arrangement of areas in its perspective projection on

[1] It should perhaps be explained, though this should be evident, that in the discussion in this book, we are not concerned with the ideas or content involved in the subject matter represented. Here, except for the consideration of formal design in tone relations, we are concerned with the methods — the grammar or rhetoric — of representation. In a discussion of complete aesthetic value in painting, we should have to take into account the matter of organization in the realm of ideas as well as the whole question of formal design, just as these matters are the main concern in a discussion of the history of art.

the retina. In this projection it is likely that no two edges are parallel. Moreover we are hardly conscious of the fact that we *see* the box by the interpretation of two different images, one for each eye; or that our visual concept is often formed on the basis of a series of such images as we move about. A mental concept of the box is formed which is quite unlike the visual image. In fact to be conscious of the visual image requires a high degree of sophistication — scientific knowledge and specially directed attention. If we were to put down our idea of an object, like a box, as simply and directly as possible on a piece of paper it is probable that we should draw the plan or the elevation of it as an Egyptian or early Greek painter would have done; or we might draw an isometric (diagonal) projection of it, like a Chinese or Japanese painter.[2] The perspective projection depends on a momentary and perhaps accidental point of view; so a geometric or isometric projection may often express more clearly our actual concept. In much drawing and painting there are distinct advantages in abstract ways of rendering the form of objects as compared with the rendering of them in perspective. For instance the scroll paintings of China and Japan could not have been conceived by artists accustomed to perspective rendering. Painters like the Egyptians and early Greeks expressed their mental concepts very clearly by representing the characteristic profiles of their objects, sometimes in plan, sometimes in elevation, and, in the case of the human figure, by combining side and front elevations of different parts of the body — the head in side profile, the eye and also the shoulders full front and so on.[3] It took a long time for

[2] An interesting illustration of what may be called the persistence of concept is found if one tries teaching a beginner to draw a cylindrical cup or glass in correct perspective. As seen below the eye the side is of course tangent to the ellipse of the base, but inevitably the student will produce an angle simply because he *knows* that in elevation there is an angle. And when he finally makes an ellipse it will probably be less instead of more wide open than the top, just as the Chinese painter, rendering his concept, will approximate an ellipse for the top of a cylindrical box and draw a horizontal line for the base.

[3] Children, of course, do this sort of thing constantly. They render their visual concepts in terms of line or area to produce pictures in which the relation of objects to each other depends on exigencies of clear representation, rather than on any actual relationship in natural space. Mr. Henry Schaefer-Simmern in *The Unfolding of Artistic Activity* recently published (Berkeley: University of California Press, 1948) shows that with children, as with primitive peoples, the early stages of the process of visual conceiving and of the rendering of concepts in the terms of drawing or painting follows under normal circumstances a regular pattern as what the author calls visual cognition is developed. In the case of the individual

Greek painters finally to become conscious of the side view of the eye. It was not until the fifteenth century that a partial understanding of the laws of perspective was acquired, and it is only in the very last few years [4] that the complete mechanics for representing objects on inclined as well as on vertical or horizontal picture planes has been worked out.[5]

Much the same thing is true in regard to the perception of tone or color. Our concepts are often far removed from the actual tones of the visual image. A person, and in particular one without special training, is inclined to interpret the tone of the various areas which make up the visual image into the facts of the local tones of the objects — that is, the tones which they exhibit when seen in full neutral light, although it is obvious that the tones projected on the retina of the eye may be very different. On a clear day snow in shadow is likely to be blue, or a red object in shadow, violet. The tones of objects in shadow or at a distance are frequently different in hue as well as in value and intensity from the tones of the same objects seen close up in ordinary light. A friend of mine looking out of the window one morning remarked on a lilac bush in blossom in the corner of a neighbor's garden that he had not noticed before. He soon observed that it was not a lilac bush but the gray-shingled roof of a shed. After that he could see the roof only as gray, and he could not be convinced that the tone he actually saw

child or untrained adult with whom his experiments have been conducted, the visual knowledge and artistic expression remain at an elementary level. The process becomes much more complicated as visual concepts and artistic expression are developed by generation after generation of artists, each adding something to the visual experience and technical expression of the preceding generation. However, the way in which visual knowledge is acquired is very much the same as at the more elementary level, only not so obvious; it is completely opposed to mere imitation of the visual image.

[4] See Stanley B. Parker, *The Vertical Vanishing Point in Linear Perspective* (Cambridge: Harvard University Press, 1947).

[5] On the other hand, the reasoning which attempts to justify the combining of parts of different "views" of objects in pictorial representation, as in much contemporary painting, by explaining that one's concept is based on views of different sides of an object and so these must be put together in a single view to form a true representation, is pure sophistry. Such paintings have nothing to do with actual visual or mental concepts. This is not to say that they have no significance at all, for the results obtained by arrangement of motives derived from the objects are often decidedly interesting as examples of formal design and also intriguing in the suggestion of subject matter after the manner of a picture puzzle. However they show a complete misapprehension of the rendering of visual concept as manifested in so much of the art of the past.

was that of lilac blossoms. When the tone was combined with more exact perception of form, he could not help translating the area on the retina of the eye into the actual fact of gray local tone. For this reason in observing a landscape in nature one is often more conscious of the actual hues and intensities projected on the eye if one turns one's head sidewise or upside down, since in this case the spatial arrangement is not so quickly interpreted into facts.

To take another instance, a white object in shadow may be a very dark gray, in deep recesses almost black, but as this tone occurs in relation to the tones of other objects also in shadow, it still appears like a white object — the mental concept is still that of a white object. However, if one looks at the white in shadow through a small hole or aperture in a piece of paper or one made by closing one's fingers over the palm of the hand, as an artist often does, one becomes conscious that the actual tone projected toward the retina of the eye is a dark gray. When teaching students in painting in a naturalistic manner, it is at first very difficult to get them to go low enough with their shadows on light objects, for they cannot at first get over the habit of translating the tones of the visual image into the facts of local tone. And it is of course only by getting down to the proper values in the shadow that one can achieve any feeling of light within the subject.

This process of observing "true" tone, as one sees it by squinting through a hole, approximates what the Report of the Colorimetry Committee of the Optical Society [6] calls "aperture color," while the ordinary interpretation or translation of the tones of the visual image into the facts of local tone is distinguished as "object color," under the general heading of modes of appearance or what might better be called modes of vision or of visual perception.

As in the case of perspective, it takes a great deal of training and knowledge to be conscious of the actual tones of the visual image projected on the retina of the eye. Accordingly primitive artists have always tended to represent merely the local tone, or "object tone," and to ignore modifications by light and shadow. They have rendered their concepts of the facts of tone.[7] Moreover Chinese and other

[6] *Op. cit.*
[7] Children of course do the same thing perfectly naturally, just as they render their spatial concepts without regard to exact visual image.

Asiatic artists persisted in this when they became far from primitive. In their painting we find flat fields of tone or a modification of these due in the main only to changes of local tone. Chinese writers defended this as a rendering of what is essential at the expense of the irrelevancy of the variations produced by light and shade, and, as we shall see later, for many purposes this, like the ignoring of perspective diminution of size, has its advantages. Likewise in earlier Renaissance painting there was usually only a slight modification of the local tone to show modeling, without any attempt to render a naturalistic effect of light. Even in Venetian painting of the sixteenth century there was always a tendency to keep whitish or light yellow draperies lighter in the shadows than would actually be the case if it had been a question of rendering the complete visual effect. The suppression of naturalistic high lights in the flesh tones in this, as in early Flemish painting and in most European painting down to the end of the eighteenth century, is another instance to illustrate the rendering of concept rather than the actual effect. It is only when we get to later nineteenth century painting, like that of Sargent, that high lights are given their literal relative value to produce, as compared with earlier painting, a sparkling superficial effect, and sometimes one that is unpleasant and even unnatural looking and greasy, since we constantly discount such high lights in every day vision.

Down through the eighteenth century little attention was paid to the possible modification of hue in shadow due to varying light effect. A red drapery usually kept its local hue, or "object hue," all the way down into shadow regardless of actual change of hue in the visual image. Except in subjects in which the lighting was simple like that of the studio or other interiors, it was not until the nineteenth century that artists like Turner and later the so-called Impressionists attempted consciously to give fully the relation of tones actually occurring in the visual image, especially in the case of more complex outdoor lighting. Apparently the Impressionists thought of it as representing the cross section of the rays of light traveling to the eye taken at the distance of the picture plane from the eye. They represented the tone of the objects modified not only by varying effects of light but also by the atmosphere through which the rays of light travel from the object to the picture plane. It was as if in looking at the subject they focused their eyes on this plane instead of changing focus according to the different distances of the objects in the more usual way of looking at things, and they used a broad, sometimes broken, method of handling which emphasized areas and suppressed exact definition of contours and details of form.

This matter of what we may call focusing of attention is another factor which determines our visual concepts. The focusing of attention on the picture plane means of course the rendering of the effect as seen at a single moment. This is quite different from the usual way in which we look at things over a space of time and quite different from the usual practice of painters in which it is assumed that the subject is represented in such a way that the attention can be focused on the separate objects represented in turn. Although closely related to the matter of aperture tone and object or local tone, two further modes of perception are really involved in this.

Likewise the different adjustment or adaptation of the eye for strong light or weak light affects our visual concepts. This again involves what might be thought of as different modes of perception. It will be considered especially in connection with the varying treatment of value relations in painting.

There are then different ways of looking at things or different *modes of perception* which to a large extent determine our visual concepts, and different types of drawing and painting depend primarily on these different kinds of concepts. But at the same time we find that much drawing and painting involves a more or less abstract way of expressing these concepts and that this is true even in painting in which the aim is to represent objects in space and light in a naturalistic manner. In other words there are different *modes of representation*, determined partly by different modes of perception and partly by the various more or less abstract ways in which the terms of drawing and painting may be used to express our concepts. Thus the concentration of the Impressionist painter on "aperture tone" may be called a mode of perception while his use of the tones of the upper surface of the tone solid in a broken or "divisionist" handling to suggest the vibration of light may be considered a variation in the mode of representation. So any use of limited ranges of hue in painting may be thought of as a matter of variation in mode of representation; also the various devices used in drawing or painting to express existence in space forward and back.

Since modes of visual perception are so closely related to modes of expression, they may be considered along with the latter in what follows.

The different types or modes of drawing and painting vary much in the manner of different languages. As we have to learn a language before we can understand what is written in it, so to understand different kinds of drawing and painting we must first know something of the different ways in which the terms of drawing and painting are used. It is only when we can understand or "read" a painting clearly and thoroughly that we are in a position to judge and appreciate it as to its artistic value. So we must first of all understand the "language" of drawing and painting, and it is the purpose of this book to assist in the attainment of this understanding.

Since what may be called the normal painting of the present day deals with the complete appearance of things, no matter whether literal or not, it will be best first of all to consider the various factors which have to be taken into account in the rendering of the total visual effect and then the manner in which these factors may be treated, or perhaps arbitrarily disregarded, in work done from different points of view.

4

THE VISUAL EFFECT

LOCAL TONES AND THEIR POSSIBLE VARIATION

Objects in nature are distinguished from each other primarily by differences of local tone.[1] In some cases, these local tones may be so transformed or overlaid by what might be called acquired tones as to be comparatively insignificant in relation to the whole effect; but under ordinary circumstances they are obviously the primary factor in the visual appearance of things.

These local tones may be modified in two principal ways: first, by the modeling of objects from light into shadow, by varying distance from the light source, or by shadows cast upon the objects; and secondly, by distance from the spectator.

GENERAL PRINCIPLE GOVERNING CHANGES OF TONE AS OBJECTS MODEL FROM LIGHT INTO SHADOW

In many paintings we are concerned with subjects like indoor scenes, still life, and so on, in which the light comes from a single source, like a window placed on one side of a room. In that case a rounded object will be strongly illuminated on the side toward the window, will be partially lighted on a part of the surface turned a little away from the window, and will be illuminated only by light reflected from other objects in the room on that part of the surface cut off from direct light, as shown in fig. 31 A. In other words it will be divided broadly into a plane of light, one of half-light, and one of shadow.

This may be shown more clearly if an object with flat sides like that shown in fig. 32 is assumed. We shall then have three definite planes of modeling.

[1] That is, the tone of an object relative to the extremes of light and dark when seen in the plane of light in the foreground — what is often called "local color," and what the physicist would call "reflectance value."

If the surface of an object is at all shiny, there may be a small portion of high light in the surface toward the light, where the light of the source itself is reflected. In a similar way there may be a deep shadow, darker than the main shadow, if some of the reflected or diffused light of the room, as well as the direct light, is cut off within the shadow, as for instance in the deeper folds of drapery.

On the whole we have to think first of all of light, half-light, and shadow, and then of the deep shadow and the high light, and possibly, as in the case of a rounded object, of intermediate tones in between the main tones.

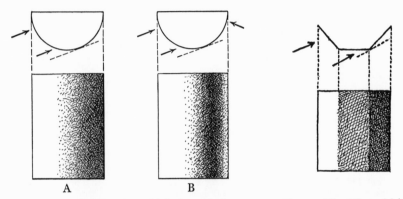

FIG. 31. The Modeling from Light into Shadow on a Cylindrical Object.

FIG. 32. The Three Main Planes of Modeling.

On a rounded object light reflected from other objects will often produce a tone on the extreme edge away from the light higher in value than that on the surface where it has just turned into shadow, as shown in fig. 31 B. This strong reflected light is made much of by a painter like Leonardo to bring out the modeling of the solid form (the idea was evidently suggested to the Florentine painters by the work of the Fleming, Van der Goes). In the work of many of Leonardo's followers this becomes a tiresome exaggeration. Beginners should be constantly on their guard not to overdo the value of the reflected light and so lose its relative darkness as compared with the plane of light.

Let us suppose that we have several flat-sided objects like that in fig. 32, each of a different "local color" or local tone, and each placed in the same way in relation to the source of light, which in this case is assumed to be neutral. One object may be RO–M, another Wt, another G–LLt, another BV–D. The value and intensity relations of the local tones in the plane of light, assuming no reflection, may be seen in fig. 33. If it is assumed for convenience that the illumination is reduced by one third in the plane of half-light, and by two thirds in the plane of shadow, the different local tones as modified in half-light and in shadow will be indicated by RO′, Wt′, G′, and BV′, and by RO″, Wt″, G″, and BV″, respectively.

This means of course a definite organization of tones as the objects model from light into shadow. With the lowering of values there is a

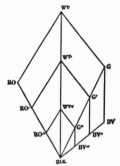

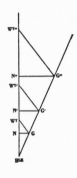

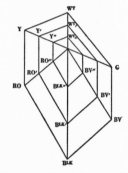

FIG. 33. The Relation of Values and Intensities in the Three Main Planes of Modeling.

FIG. 34. The Relation of Values and Intensities as Objects are Brought from Darkness into Light.

FIG. 35. The Relation of Values and Intensities as Objects Recede into Distance.

proportional lowering of values and intensities. Although the contrasts between the tones are reduced with the approach to blackness, the relation between the tones stays the same. It is a *proportional diminution of contrasts*. In deep shadow the tones may approach closer to black; in high light each tone will come between the local tone in the plane of light and the tone of the light — thus, in the diagram (fig. 33) in which Wt is assumed to be an ideal white, the high light in the case of the RO will come on the line RO–Wt.

This may be illustrated by making a diagram similar to fig. 32, with stripes of various local tones painted across the object, and with these local tones lowered in value and intensity according to the diagram of values and intensities in fig. 33, to show the proportional diminution of contrasts. If this is accurately made, a convincing effect of modeling in light and shade will be produced. It is a very good exercise for beginners in the study of tone relations.

This may be illustrated in reverse fashion by means of bits of drapery varying in local tone. Suppose that we have a white, a black, and a gray drapery, and a green drapery of the same value as the gray. If we go with these into a closet and shut the door, we have zero of illumination, and zero of value and intensity, represented in fig. 34 by Blk. If we open the door to let in a little light, we begin to distinguish between the tones. In this light we might represent them by Wt, Blk, G, and N, assuming that the Blk is an ideal black and does not reflect any light, as it certainly would in the case of any actual drapery, and leaving out of account also some actual change of relative value and hue, as the eye adapts itself to a higher or lower degree of general illumination. If we come out of the closet and toward the window, still making the same assumptions, the Wt may come up to Wt'. In that case the N will come up in value to correspond, and the G will increase in both value and intensity in proportion. Near the window all the tones will move up and out still farther.[2]

This law of proportional diminution of contrasts may be considered a general principle governing the changes of tone as objects model from light into shadow. If another light source is added, the principle still holds, but its operation becomes somewhat more complicated. With several light sources the organization frequently becomes too complicated for visual appreciation, and although modern painters have sometimes found novel interest in the harmony of the angular shapes of shadows resulting from multiple light sources, the subjects we ordinarily find more interesting are those in which the orderly relation of tones is definitely appreciable.

The same principle applies of course as objects are placed nearer or farther in relation to the light source, as in a room with the light

[2] This at least approximates what actually happens. But, as hinted above, there is considerable change in relative value and hue as general illumination is increased or decreased. This has practically no significance in the modeling of objects from light into shadow in the ordinary room illumination, where the eye stays adapted, to one general illumination; but it has a good deal to do with the varied effect of tone in twilight or evening subjects. In subdued light the eye is relatively more sensitive to light at the blue end of the spectrum than in normal daylight. (Psychologists know this as the Purkinje effect.) This may be observed by looking at the large color chart (Plate LXIX), in a much darkened room. The blues will all

coming from a window at one side. Objects far from the window will be less highly illuminated than those near, and values and intensities will diminish or increase in proportion to the illumination.

Qualifications

The exact working of this law according to the simple diagram shown in fig. 33 is of course interfered with in certain instances. These are principally in the case of the light itself being colored, or of light being reflected from colored objects, and in the case of shiny surfaces which reflect the tones of other objects.

If the light is colored, a proportional change in hue toward the hue of the light will accompany the changes in value and intensity as the object models into the light. This may be definitely felt and may be rendered in painting; but the graphic expression of the change would require a three-dimensional diagram, and it is sufficient if we understand the principle involved. In the case of two or three sources of light, there may be differences of hue between these, and the problem is complicated still more; but the general principle will hold just the same.

The tone of shadows may frequently be changed in hue or in intensity of hue by reflection of light from some other object. For instance a yellow drapery with its shadow side turned toward the light side of a red drapery will change to an orange in the shadow.[3] In ordinary indoor subjects such changes are not usually very great, and they modify the general arrangement of tones only slightly. In landscape the effect may be much more significant.

The qualifications are greater in the case of shiny surfaces, for in this case the tone of objects reflected in a surface may be of more importance than the local tone of the object. This is especially true in the

---

seem relatively lighter and the warm tones relatively darker than in ordinary light. Such a chart made in the light of a late afternoon will show defects in the adjustment of value relations when seen in brighter light the next day. For this reason it is not safe to paint in declining light.

[3] In a similar way the purity and hence the relative intensity of the tone of shadow in the folds of a drapery may be somewhat increased by the reflection of light from an illuminated surface of the same drapery. The same thing is true in the case of other surfaces as well as that of drapery if the light is reflected into the shadow from a surface of the same local tone. This is due to the fact that there is more perfect subtraction when the light is reflected back and forth from surface to surface.

case of water surfaces in outdoor subjects. The final tone in any given case will be a combination of the local tone of the water and of the tone of the object reflected in the surface; the result will be determined by the relative strength of the light coming from the two sources and by the angle of reflection. If the water is highly illuminated, as by sunlight, the local tone of the water will count more, especially in those parts of the surface where dark objects are reflected — in this case we can look down into the water and see its tone, or that of the bottom if the water is shallow; but the local tone of the water will count for less when it is not strongly illuminated or where very light objects, like cloud or sky or white sails in light, are reflected in the surface.[4]

In landscape, reflection also frequently plays a prominent part in the case of surfaces that are not as reflective as water surfaces. Thus on clear days snow in shadow is usually very reflective of the tone of the sky — hence the blue shadows on snow on sunny days. As a matter of fact almost every object when in shadow is more or less reflective of the tone of the sky, and there is considerable change in the hue of local tones of objects in landscape as they pass from light into shadow, although the general principle of proportional diminution of contrasts holds true, especially in the foreground. It is partly because of this, and partly because of the change effected in the tones of objects as they recede into the distance until a thick layer of air is placed between them and the observer, that the exact rendering of local tones of objects in landscape painting becomes a matter of minor importance in comparison with the general relation of warm and cool tones, the essential effect of which can often be rendered very simply, as suggested in Chapters 7 and 8.

In spite of these qualifications, the law of proportional diminution of contrasts is nevertheless the first important general principle governing the visual effect. In most cases the qualifications in the working of the simple law are relatively of small importance.

[4] The general principles governing reflection in water surfaces are discussed very fully in the first volume of Ruskin's *Modern Painters*; and although the treatment might perhaps have been made more thoroughly scientific, there is, so far as I know, no other place where the subject is so well handled, especially in the matter of keen observation and clear description of natural effect.

THE GENERAL PRINCIPLE GOVERNING CHANGES OF TONE AS
OBJECTS RECEDE FROM THE FOREGROUND INTO
THE DISTANCE

A somewhat similar proportional diminution of contrasts takes place in the case of objects receding into the distance. This applies particularly to landscape in which there is a great difference between foreground and distant planes; but in painting the principle is sometimes made use of in an arbitrary way to distinguish planes forward and back even in subjects much more limited in depth.

The simplest possible case might be explained by means of the diagram in fig. 35. Suppose that we have objects of the local tones RO, Y, Wt, G, BV, and Blk; and suppose that these are to be seen at different distances in a thick gray fog or mist, the relative value of which is Lt. The values of the other tones are indicated in the diagram. In the foreground the local tones of the various objects will not be affected; but as they are carried part way back into the distance the

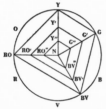

FIG. 36. The Relation of Hues and Intensities as Objects Recede into Distance.
The local tone of the air is here assumed to be neutral.

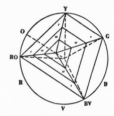

FIG. 37. The Relation of Hues and Intensities as Objects Recede into Distance.
The local tone of the air is here assumed to be orange of low intensity.

local tones will be definitely overlaid with the gray of the mist and will appear at a certain distance as RO′, Y′, etc. In a plane still farther back they will appear as RO″, Y″, etc.; and still farther back they may finally be completely swallowed up in the gray of the fog. This might be shown also in the circular diagram of hues and intensities, as in fig. 36. Differences of value, as in the case of Wt and Blk, cannot of course be shown in this diagram.

As in modeling from light into shadow, the diminution of contrasts is proportional.

Suppose that the thick fog, instead of being gray, were a low intensity of orange, as shown in fig. 37; the diminution of contrasts would still be proportional, but there would be changes in hue as well as of intensity and value in the tone of the different fields.

Qualifications

The effect shown in fig. 35 would probably be possible in the case of a thick fog, and even that shown in fig. 37 might be possible in certain circumstances; but they would at least be rare and not at all those with which we are concerned in most landscape painting. Although there are obvious changes in hue, as well as in value and intensity, as objects recede into the distance in almost all landscape subjects, and although these changes are easily felt to be lawful, they can hardly be represented completely in graphic diagrams. This is due to the complication introduced by the different ways in which long and short wave lengths are transmitted through dense atmosphere. On account of this variation darker objects will tend to change in hue toward blue or blue-violet, and lighter objects will turn toward yellow, or orange, or red.

This is due to the phenomenon known as scattering of light, or we might, more simply, call it *selection of long and short wave lengths*.[5] The reason for this is that in air containing finely divided dust particles — there is always a certain amount of such particles, but it varies very considerably — the rays of light of short wave length are more easily turned from their course than those of longer wave length; hence the short wave lengths are partly deflected, and some of them even reflected back toward the original source of light, while the longer ones are transmitted through the atmosphere without such deflection or with comparatively little.[6]

The best example of this phenomenon is to be found in the case of thin wood smoke, a column of which seen over a dark background, with the light in this case coming mainly from the direction of the observer, appears bluish in tone, while the same column seen against the

[5] The longer wave lengths come of course at the red end of the spectrum and the shorter at the blue and violet end.

[6] For an explanation of the complete scientific theory involved in this, the reader will have to refer to books on the physics of light.

sky, with the light coming mainly from the opposite side through the smoke toward the observer, appears brownish or orange.[7] Here there is only a thin layer of many finely divided particles, but the same general thing happens in the case of thick layers of air in which there are more or less dust particles suspended. The greater the number of particles, the greater will be the differentiation of warm and cool tones. Hence the blue of distant hills (in this case the direction of the dominant light is away from the observer toward the dark background), the relative warmth of sky or of cloud directly above the hills (in this case the direction of the dominant light is toward the observer), hence also in all probability the usual bluish hue of the sky. On a smoky day in autumn the sunlight itself becomes very warm in tone, as opposed to the bluish tones of the shadows. The contrast of warm and cool tones becomes stronger ordinarily at sunset, when the sun's rays travel slantwise through layers of dust-laden air. Hills and clouds in shadow then become very strong in blue, or blue-violet, and the sky and illuminated clouds become orange or pink or red. In spite of all these variations, the tones are all organized by the working of an absolutely definite law and are felt to be so.[8]

As mentioned before, this frequently produces an effect in landscape in which the variations of local tone are of minor significance compared with the general atmospheric scheme; but the fundamental principle of diminution of contrasts of local tones with distance holds good here as in the earlier examples, and in the usual landscape subject will count for a good deal, especially in the foreground and middle distances. Relative to the light of the sky most objects in landscape in ordinary daylight are comparatively dark, and, except for rather violent sunset effects, these will all tend in greater or less degree toward a gray-blue in the distance. Only very light objects, like clouds seen in light, will tend toward positively warm tone.

[7] The same effect is often produced by tobacco smoke. The degree of selection depends in part on the fineness of the particles.

[8] Henry Rutgers Marshall in his book called *The Beautiful* (London, 1924) says that he can imagine no "appreciation of relations" (in other words, of organization) in connection with the beauty of a sunset! I think we may imagine it very easily. It is the whole thing.

CAST SHADOWS

Aside from the modeling of objects in light and shade, and the variation of tone with distance, shadows cast by one object on other objects play a part in the visual effect. The resulting tone depends on the same principle as the diminution of contrasts with modeling, or on this combined with the variation of tone with distance, as in the case of all shadow. It is only necessary to mention this here because in much actual painting of the past, as in most of that in Italy before the sixteenth century, modeling of individual surfaces was taken into account, though not in a naturalistic manner, while the matter of cast shadows was completely ignored.

PERSPECTIVE PROJECTION

In the complete visual effect the positions, measures, and shapes of the various areas of the visual image depend partly on the actual arrangement of the objects, and partly on the way in which these are projected upon the retina of the eye, or upon a corresponding picture plane, by means of rays of light which converge on a single point. This is known as conic projection or perspective projection.

This needs to be mentioned as one of the factors in the visual effect only because in a good deal of painting other methods of projection are used in place of perspective projection. In architectural renderings, for example, the plan and elevation representing a building are based on geometric projection — cylindric instead of conic — and, as suggested in Chapter 3, this method, or something approaching it, has often been used in other kinds of painting, as in that of Greece and Egypt. Although ignoring the superficial appearance of things, it is just as accurate a way of showing the form of objects as perspective projection — in fact it is sometimes clearer, as in the case of the architectural drawing, to anyone who is trained to read it.

Still another kind of projection is used in Chinese and Japanese painting. For want of a better word this may be called diagonal projection (it is not strictly speaking isometric). The projection in this case is by means of parallel lines inclined both vertically and horizontally to the picture plane. This means that an accurate rendering of space forward and back may be made, but nearer objects come lower and farther ones higher on the plane of the picture. There is no diminution in size as in perspective; the sides of rectangular objects running back from the picture plane are shown by inclined lines which are parallel instead of converging on a vanishing point as in perspective. In any strict use of this method the depth of space that can be shown is limited by the height of the picture. This is illustrated by many of the scrolls and screens, as shown in Plate I. In landscape the Chinese and Japanese painters often get around this limitation of space by a perspective-like diminution in size from plane to plane, while within each plane objects are shown in the diagonal manner.[9] This kind of projection is usually used very freely in all Asiatic painting — that is, without much regard for scientific accuracy; but, especially in Chinese and Japanese art, the description of form and of space is perfectly readable to anyone who gets used to the convention of it. In many ways it is just as reasonable to use as perspective. It is another system of projection, rather than merely a primitive attempt at perspective, as it so often is called.

In other types of painting the representation of space forward and back is almost completely ignored. In the decorative altarpieces of the fourteenth century, for example, the figures were treated as so many elements of pattern in silhouette, to be arranged on the flat surface of the panel as exigencies of design and of expression of religious idea might dictate, without any concern for their actual volume. In relation to the architectural function of this particular kind of painting this was altogether appropriate and satisfactory. The same treatment is found in much Persian painting, which also was primarily a matter of decoration, only in this case of the surface of a page in a book.

[9] In large landscape paintings of the hanging or *kakemono* type, an ascending viewpoint is often employed. That is, the foreground is represented as if one were fairly low, the middle distance as if one were somewhat higher, perhaps halfway up a very high tower, and the distance as if one were at the top of the tower. An approach to this manner of representing space is to be seen in some of Dürer's woodcuts where a higher horizon is assumed for the landscape than for the foreground figures and buildings.

THE DIFFERENT FACTORS TO BE CONSIDERED IN THE
RENDERING OF THE TOTAL VISUAL EFFECT

We may sum up the preceding discussion by saying that the following principal factors must be considered in the representation of the total visual effect:

1. The local tones of the different objects.

2. The modification of the local tones by modeling from light into shadow, or by distance from the light source.

3. The modification of the local tones by distance from the spectator.

4. Cast shadows.

5. Perspective projection.

(Items 2 and 3 are qualified as explained above.)

All these factors must be considered in painting in which it is aimed to represent the complete appearance of things, that is, the appearance of objects as existing in light and space beyond a picture plane; but in painting that still may be perfectly understandable certain of these factors can be entirely disregarded.

We may now proceed to what we may call the different methods or modes of representation. These will be concerned with the visual effect in varying degrees; but on the basis of our understanding of the general principles governing the visual effect, it will be easier to understand the significance of the various abstractions employed in different periods and phases of art.

The modes of representation may be broadly, if arbitrarily, distinguished between painting and drawing according to whether or not the element of color (hue and intensity) is included. It may be added, however, that in everyday practice it is convenient to use the term drawing to include examples in which some suggestion of color is added but where the emphasis is on form, as in the sixteenth-century portrait drawings of François Clouet, done in red and black and sometimes also yellow and white chalks.

5

THE MODES OF DRAWING

The Modes of Drawing may be distinguished as *delineation* (line drawing), *form drawing*, and *color-value drawing*. Pure line drawing is rather rare, for line is usually used in combination with other kinds of drawing and painting, as in the mode of line and local tone found in most Oriental painting. Moreover in drawings which are mainly a matter of modeling in light and shadow a certain amount of the form is often expressed by means of delineation. Drawings, therefore, cannot all be classified precisely into these three types; there may be many variations within the types, or combinations of the types. Nevertheless the classification into these principal modes is a convenience for a clear understanding of the possibilities of expression in drawing, and as a general basis for the judging of quality in examples of this art.

In a general way these modes may be defined as follows. In the *mode of delineation* form is expressed entirely by line. There is ordinarily no direct reference to light and shadow in this use of line, but expression of relative distance of planes forward and back may be achieved by varying the width or depth of lines to indicate stronger contrasts in near planes in comparison with lesser contrasts in farther planes, and the relative connection and disconnection of planes forward and back may be indicated by various conventions.

In the *mode of form drawing* there is expression of the relative illumination of surface entirely without regard to the values of the local tones of the different objects. In the drawing of single objects or figures, as in much Renaissance figure drawing, this becomes a sculpturesque manner of drawing, one used for the study of plastic form without regard to general light effect. On the other hand, in the drawings of Rembrandt, Ostade, and other Dutch masters, and in those of Tiepolo, there is more often a rendering of general light effect. Naturally expression of relative illumination of surface in this way, often with more or less abstraction into broad areas of light and shadow, is frequently supplemented by delineation.

In the *mode of color-value drawing* not only is there expression of the relative illumination of surface, but there is also expression of the differences of value in the local tones of the various objects. Color-value drawing thus approaches the mode of expression found in complete painting. Differences in rendering corresponding to the different modes of painting might actually be produced in this mode; but as a matter of fact color-value drawing was first developed in the art of line engraving in the seventeenth century, in which the purpose was to reproduce, as far as was possible in black and white, the effect of complete painting; so in most examples of color-value drawing actually produced in the past the aim has been to render the complete effect of illumination along with the values of the local tones.

Delineation was relied on for the expression of form in almost all Asiatic art, in Egyptian and earlier Greek art, and in much Byzantine and medieval art, especially where the Asiatic influence was strong. In the Renaissance, also, much reliance was placed on line for the expression of form, although there was usually some modeling of surface as well.

Most of the later medieval and Renaissance drawings are in the mode of form drawing. Drawings were made especially for the study of specific form in nature, or, in the later Renaissance, for the study of general distribution of light and shadow in sketches for complete paintings. Engravings of the earlier Renaissance were also made almost exclusively in this mode.

As pointed out above, the mode of color-value drawing was not extensively employed until the seventeenth century, and from that time on it was employed especially in reproductive engraving after paintings. The art of reproductive engraving was finally "put out of business" by the photograph and the photo-mechanical engraving processes. A photograph is of course a rendering in the mode of color value. Modern artists have used this mode more or less, but often in a modified form, as will be explained later on.

DELINEATION

Expression of Three-dimensional Form

A large volume would have to be written to discuss fully the possibilities of expression in line drawing, and to point out clearly the fundamental differences between good and commonplace or bad use of line. On account of the general limits of this volume we must confine ourselves here to a brief indication of the main points to be considered.

All delineation is of course abstract, and it has little to do with the popular notion of imitation of superficial effect; but because line drawings are easily read by almost anyone, this abstraction is usually not thought much about. There are obviously no lines in nature; there are only areas of tone distinguished from each other by contrasts at their edges. The extension and shape of objects are ordinarily most strikingly marked by these edges, and so when we indicate the position and shape of these by lines we express the general form of objects to some extent. Thus by silhouettes which show merely the limiting outline of the contrasting edges of the object we may at least infer a good deal of the idea of solid form. Within the outline of almost every object, however, there is also a variety of planes, and these planes often meet in edges. If we draw lines to define the position and shape of these edges, or contours, we express more of the form of the object. In groups of objects, or in single objects that have projecting parts, like the arms and legs of a figure, there are usually different planes forward and back, and parts of the object or objects in the farther planes are cut off by those in the nearer planes. If we distinguish in some way between these different planes forward and back, especially by emphasizing the continuity of the edges or lines within each plane and their disconnection from the lines of farther planes, we express still more of the form. Moreover some edges are more significant in connection with the form of an object as a whole than other edges; so we may discriminate between those that are important and those that are unimportant, leaving out unimportant ones, if necessary, in order that they may not interfere with the expressiveness of the important ones, or emphasizing and accenting the more important lines, at the expense

of the less important. In some cases the time taken to make a drawing
may determine how much is to be put in. Besides, in drawing, as well
as in speech, brevity is frequently the soul of wit.

All this requires a great deal of judgment, and in general it is this
judgment in the selection and organization of the lines employed to
express the solid form which distinguishes good from commonplace
examples of draftsmanship.[1]

Many superb examples of the use of line to express solid form are to
be found among the drawings by the great masters of the Renaissance.
In these the expression depends partly on the subtle adjustment of the
shapes of lines, perhaps on either side of a leg or an arm, to suggest the
solid form between. An inferior draftsman may draw the line of the
side of an object to make it correspond fairly well to the original edge,
but will tend to forget its subtle relation to the opposite edge of the
object. The result is a disorganization of line and a flatness of form.
A real master will draw every line of an object not only to give the
form of the immediate detail, but also to express its relation to the total
form of the object. It is this complete organization which explains the
aesthetic interest which we find in the slightest drawings of the great
masters. To achieve it is not so easy as it sounds offhand.

The distinction between the work of a master and that of a
mediocre artist in this particular is to be observed in the two drawings
shown in Plate II, one by Pollaiuolo and the other by an inferior follower of his "school." Superficially they are similar in style; but one is
a mannered drawing of individual lines without consideration for their
relation to one another; the other is an amazingly convincing rendering
of solid form.

In the detail of the shoulder and torso (Plate III) Pollaiuolo has
used the device met with constantly in the work of accomplished

[1] In this connection Mr. R. D. Feild has called my attention to the following
passage from Pliny: "Parrhasios first gave painting symmetry . . . by the verdict
of artists he is unrivalled in the rendering of outline. This is the highest subtlety
obtainable in painting. Merely to paint a figure in relief is no doubt a great
achievement, yet many have succeeded thus far. But where an artist is rarely
successful is in finding an outline which shall express the contours of a figure. For
the contour should appear to fold back, and so to enclose the object as to give
assurance of the parts behind, thus suggesting even what it conceals. Preëminence
in this respect is conceded to Parrhasios by Antigonos and Xenokrates, writers on
painting, who indeed not only concede but insist upon it." *The Elder Pliny's
Chapters on the History of Art*, trans. by K. Jex-Blake (London, 1896), pp. 111, 113.

artists. The line in the nearer plane is made a continuous stroke, distinct from the stroke in the farther plane, regardless of what the mere outline of the figure may be. Sometimes there is a considerable space left where one line goes behind another so that there may be no confusion of planes. This might be spoken of as a *marking of the connection and disconnection of planes* forward and back. It is seen in the Pollaiuolo in the drawing of the muscular form under the arm. Pollaiuolo has drawn not merely the outline of the body as might logically be done; he has suggested the surfaces of the series of muscles, and hence the form of the whole body, by showing the lines passing around and in back of those in front. In this way one is made to feel the whole form clearly.[2] The same clear distinction of planes is to be seen throughout the drawing — in the way in which the arm holds its place in front of the body, in the drawing of the knee, and obviously in the drawing of the head of the axe on which the figure is leaning. In contrast with this there is almost no suggestion of planes in the "school" drawing. The lines indicating the fingers of the left hand, actually disappearing under the right arm, are in precisely the same plane as the line of the arm. And there is no thought of the form of the figure as a whole in the drawing of the continuous wavy line down the side of the torso and leg. These two drawings make an extreme contrast — the "school" drawing is probably a copy by some inferior apprentice, possibly retouched at a later time; nevertheless they are typical as illustrations of the difference constantly to be observed between the work of the master and that of the "school."

A few other drawings are reproduced in Plates IV–XV, to illustrate this same point. In the Pinturicchio the planes of the mass of folds sweeping around the figure and passing under the arm are clearly distinguished. The disappearance of one fold under another is always

---

[2] So far as the art of drawing goes this is probably the principal factor in what Berenson calls the rendering of "tactile values" which requires on the part of the artist a complete grasp and visualization of the three-dimensional form. Berenson's explanation of this by reference to the sense of touch seems to me somewhat misleading. The organization of the subject itself and also of the lines or strokes in a drawing is apprehended visually. Compare *Gestalt Psychology*, by Wolfgang Köhler (New York, 1929), p. 220. That one can *feel* the structure and solidity is perhaps a description, but it is hardly an explanation of the distinguishing character of the drawing.

distinctly marked.[3] In the drawing by Raphael (Plate V) after a figure in an engraving by Mantegna, note the complicated "in-and-outness" of the lines which draw the folds of drapery over the left arm of the figure, and the clear fashion in which the whole arm stands out in relation to the body in back. An extremely sensitive use of the device is to be seen in the drawing of the reclining nude figure by Rubens (Plate VI), which is an example of straight delineation unusual for a master of the seventeenth century. In the Toba Sojo (Plate VII) large breaks between the nearer and farther lines are frequently made to distinguish the planes, and the lines are freely accented by variations in width to bring out the most important contours or spots. The detail from the drawing by Rembrandt or by one of his pupils (Plate VIII), striking in its likeness to the Toba Sojo, illustrates a much more rapid handling and more vigorous breaking of the lines in the different planes. Very obvious examples are to be found occasionally in the illustrations by artists who have worked in the general tradition exemplified in *Punch*, where the device of dropping the line in the more distant plane on either side of the nearer object is used consistently to make the drawing "read" as clearly as possible.[4] Often the breaks are unbelievably wide. Very obvious use of the device is also occasionally found in cartoons and drawings in newspapers and magazines in this country.

The detail of the drawing of Edinburgh by Turner (Plate IX) illustrates the principle of omission of detail for the sake of emphasis of the main contours of the successive planes. This is essentially the same device as that used in most Chinese landscape paintings, or drawings, in India ink (Plate X). In these the detail is crowded together and the washes darkened toward the top of each succeeding plane of mountain or hill to bring it out against the space left purposely blank in the lower part of the plane beyond. The omission of detail in the farther plane in each case frequently suggests the idea of mist in the valley (the same is true in the Turner drawing), but it is really a more or less arbitrary device to bring out the different planes forward and back. In the Chinese painting or drawing in India ink it is of course

[3] Follow down the right edge of this drawing, and note how it is built up out of contours all clearly distinguished in plane.

[4] An amusing instance is to be observed in the Picasso etching reproduced on our title page; here the outline of the face is omitted entirely so as to avoid confusion with the line of the canvas in the nearer plane.

only occasionally that straight delineation is employed; nevertheless the principles and methods involved are almost exactly the same as in the pure line drawing of the Turner.

A use of the same arbitrary device for expression of planes forward and back in the Ch'ên Jung Dragon Scroll (Plate LVII) is discussed in the succeeding chapter, where it is pointed out that much of the arbitrariness of expression of abstract delineation is to be found even in Venetian painting of the sixteenth century. This merely illustrates how much there is that is arbitrary and abstract in all drawing and painting, especially before the introduction of the imitative point of view in the nineteenth century.

The use of lighter lines in the distance to indicate the diminishing contrasts in the farther planes is illustrated in the Prout drawing of Evreux (Plate XI), and also in the etching of Ben Arthur from Turner's *Liber Studiorum* (Plate XIII). The dropping of the lines in the farther planes so as not to disturb the continuity of contour and the feeling of "wholeness" in the nearer objects is also well illustrated in the Prout, where the lines are dropped off entirely in the lower part of the tower to make it carry beyond the roofs of the houses in the foreground. Prout has introduced the device of smoke in this case to make the break even greater. The distinction of planes is perhaps less obvious, but it is even more complete in the Turner. In the torrent bed at the left, for example, one can follow — almost clamber back — from stone to stone up the slope without hesitation, for each line is definitely placed in its proper plane of distance. The same manner of distinguishing planes forward and back is shown also in Turner's drawing of an Alpine subject (Plate XII). Note especially the omission of detail beyond the bridge.

The difference between the work of the master and that of the school, illustrated before in the case of Pollaiuolo, is exemplified in a comparison of another etching from the *Liber Studiorum* (Plate XIV) with the "Ben Arthur" (Plate XIII). Except for a small passage in the lower right corner evidently executed by Turner's own hand, this plate was etched after Turner's sketch of the subject by the engraver who usually did only the final mezzotinting of the plates. In the passage of slopes covered with fir trees in the middle distance there is merely a mannered repetition of lines that is completely flat in spite of the clumsy white area left around the outline of the nearer trees. The engraver had not the power of imaginative vision to handle this passage properly.

Another example which shows a crowding of detail toward the top edge of each plane with omission of detail beyond is seen in the landscape drawing by Brueghel (Plate XV). This may be compared with the landscape scroll by Tung Yüan to show how similar were the means employed which distinguish the best drawing of both western and eastern artists. In the Brueghel, as also occasionally in Chinese ink "paintings," sometimes an area of lighter tone is distinguished against a darker area beyond which is crowded with detail. This gives a pleasant interchange; a similar device is also used sometimes in paintings by Cézanne.

In all of this we have subtle and complex organization of line — an organization in the terms of the drawing itself. We describe our reaction to this ordinarily by saying that the objects are convincingly solid or that the space is clearly expressed, just as in the case of a painting by Vermeer we describe our reaction to the organization of the tones by saying that there is convincing rendering of space and atmosphere; but it is the expressive organization of the terms themselves that is fundamental.

The Use of Abstract Line Motives

Another instance of abstraction in line drawing is seen in the usual way in which complicated detail, as in landscape, is interpreted, or transposed one might say, into certain sets of pencil or brush strokes which render what seem to the artist the essential features of the form without in any way representing it in an imitative fashion. Some of the best examples of this are found in the treatment of foliage in Chinese and Japanese painting. The landscape by Sesson (Plate XVI) is a good illustration. The bamboo is interpreted by means of a repetition of strokes that by their wedge-shaped character suggest the shape of the bamboo leaves. These are varied considerably to indicate varying degrees of foreshortening, and are so arranged as to express the essential order of the form — the gradations in direction and in measure from the lower to the upper part of the stem, along with the general harmony or uniformity of shape and measure — and to render clearly the action of the branches as they are bent back by the strong wind, without the least attempt to give anything like the exact number of details that there would be in the subject itself. The character of the touch is changed to represent other kinds of foliage, and the tree with the bare stems is represented by means of a repetition of strokes of the brush which indicate the harmony of shape and measure in the branches and stems of the tree, with no suggestion of exact naturalism. It is a transposition from the terms of nature into the terms of drawing: in nature the organization of form is rendered in details of countless leaves and twigs and branches; in drawing the same general organization of detail is expressed, but by means of strokes of the brush or pencil which are related in size and number to the general character of the drawing as a whole. Constantly detail is rendered in this abstract fashion in Chinese and Japanese painting or drawing. A variety of linear terms is employed — a great number of different kinds of strokes for representing rock form, and a large variety of line motives to represent other kinds of detail, such as waves, foam, cloud, smoke, flame, locks of hair, folds of drapery. These are developed freely within individual compositions according to the immediate requirements, but they form nevertheless a definite vocabulary. There is a close analogy between the use of these linear motives in Oriental painting and the use of motives in music, like that of Wagner, to suggest the general character of motion in water or in flame.

In the West, also, landscape detail is frequently interpreted in purely abstract line motives. The Venetian masters of the early sixteenth century may not have invented but they at least did much to develop a regular set of linear terms for the rendering of foliage. In their use of a series of rounded, scalloped strokes to indicate the essential radiation of the details in masses of foliage enclosed in bounding graded curves, they set a precedent which was followed by almost all Western landscape draftsmen down to the middle of the nineteenth century. A particularly varied use of such conventional strokes, adapted from Claude and Poussin, is found in the etchings of Turner's *Liber Studiorum* (Plate XVII). The general measure of stroke used to indicate detail in a drawing must necessarily harmonize with the measure of stroke used in the drawing as a whole. Fine lines cannot be used in one place and coarse in another without disturbing the general harmony of effect, unless there may be some definite gradation of touch from foreground to distance. Dürer and Holbein understood this well, as is shown in their woodcuts.

Expressionism

Another instance of abstract rendering in the mode of delineation is the use of line, found especially in the work of Chinese and Japanese artists, to produce a definite emotional effect. Obvious examples of this are seen in some of the later Japanese paintings and prints. In Plate XVIII, for instance, a print by Torii Kiyomasu, an actor is shown taking the part of a man in a towering passion. The whole mood of the picture is enhanced immeasurably by the use of short jagged strokes — lines of rage — in much of the drawing, and by the general angular character of the form. This angularity is of course partly a matter of pose and costume, but in addition the stroking is deliberately emotional in intent. A striking contrast to this is seen in the representation of the priest Hotei (Plate XIX), who for the Chinese and Japanese was a sort of symbol of contentment. He was supposed to have gone about the world perfectly carefree, begging his food from door to door, and filling his sack with what he didn't put into his big round belly at the moment. In this drawing the lines are principally big sweeping curves — lines of contented motion. A much more subtle emotional effect, but none the less definite, was obtained by Harunobu in his print of the female figure floating away on a scroll (Plate XX). There is a charming harmony from the point of view of formal design in the repetition of the flowing sinuous line throughout the composition; but still more important is the suggestion of gentle mood that this line conveys. The variation of stroke in these different works suggests the difference of stroke employed by a violinist in playing passages which vary in mood — the sharp, abrupt bowing for the stormy passages, the graceful, flowing movements for the more sentimental passages. The difference in bowing is of course essential for the proper result in sound, but even visually the varying action is expressive of the changing moods of a composition. This is one reason why a musical performance seems to lack in completeness when it is heard over the radio or on the phonograph.

Much grander examples of emotional expression are found in some of the earlier Buddhistic paintings, as in the early Japanese painting of a Bodhisattva (Plate XXI). Here in the slight outward and upward trend of the petals of the lotus throne, in the upward movement of the flame motives around the large halo, in the swelling curve of the halo itself, in the surging, waving flames of the small halo and the smaller flame motives used throughout the ornaments of the figure, there is conveyed a sense of spiritual elevation and exaltation that becomes almost overpowering as one looks at the picture intently. This mystical expression achieved by the use of abstract line motives is characteristic of the Buddhistic painting of both China and Japan. A similar use of line for emotional effect is to be found occasionally also in Western painting, especially in that which approaches mystical expression, as in the work of Simone Martini or of Botticelli.

Calligraphic Quality

Occasionally both in Western and Oriental art, expression of form in a naturalistic or expressionistic fashion has been subordinated to a definitely ornamental use of line. Such drawing is usually described as calligraphic, in that the emphasis on superficial harmony of size and shape of stroke is like that found in fine pieces of writing, or that the strokes of the drawing approach in character the ornamental flourishes of the accomplished penman. In the East there has always been a close connection between the art of writing and that of painting and drawing, for the technique involved in the manipulation of the brush is the same in both cases. Fine pieces of writing have always been prized as having, from the formal point of view, the same value as paintings; and drawing and painting have always preserved something of the superficial convention of writing — its ornamental character. In later medieval art in the West, this leaning toward a superficially ornamental, rather than purely expressionistic, manner is particularly noticeable. In the art of the so-called "international style" of the end of the fourteenth and the beginning of the fifteeth century, there is shown a liking for graceful, sinuous curves, which give a charming ornamental effect, entirely independent of any intent of expression of actual movement. In the work of the German engravers of the sixteenth century the calligraphic character is carried still further. In much of the wood and copper engraving of these artists the effect is one of purely decorative covering of the area of the composition — it is the primary consideration in the mind of the artist.[5]

In an ideal example of form drawing there would be no reference whatever to the value of the local tones (this is what is ordinarily meant by the term "color-value"), but the relative illumination of the different surfaces would be rendered fully and exactly. It could be made without resort to any delineation.

As a matter of fact such a drawing is rarely seen. The regular art-school drawing in charcoal from a cast usually presents the features of such a drawing, but in this the omission of color-value takes place in the rendering into the uniform tone of the plaster in the making of the cast itself, and it is not a deliberate omission on the part of the student, who probably thinks of his performance in most cases as a color-value drawing of a white object. In the work of the great masters, to which I am principally referring, the omission of color-value is deliberate, and in such drawing there is usually some use of delineation, at least to mark the limits of the object or objects against the background on the light side. Frequently lines are used to accent the main contours or to indicate detail, as of locks of hair, even where the modeling of surface is pretty complete. The drawings by Lorenzo di Credi and by Michelangelo shown in Plates XXII and XXIII come about as near to pure form drawing as any usually found. Often there is much more reliance on delineation, with a very summary indication of the main distribution of light and shadow.

In the engraving by Schongauer (Plate XXIV) the modeling of the individual fields is shown without regard to color-value and, as in painting in the mode of relief, without reference to cast shadows or general effect of light. The sculpturesque effect of such a composition is common to most of the early line engravings of the fifteenth and sixteenth centuries, and a similar idea of rendering sculpturesque form

[5] In most of these drawings there is shading to express modeling or light-effect as well as delineation; in this case the calligraphic quality is extended to the lines used in shading. In fact the matter of design in the touch employed throughout a work is one of the fundamental interests in the drawings and even in the paintings of the great masters of the Renaissance.

is at the bottom of most of the figure drawings of the Renaissance. Indeed much of the painting in the mode of relief might be looked upon as mere form drawing in monochrome, only with the color used changed from field to field.

On the other hand, in the drawings by Rembrandt and Tiepolo (Plates XXV and XXVI), there is expression of broad effect of light and shadow in extended subjects, and this is found constantly in the studies for pictures made by the Venetian and later Renaissance painters, who put so much emphasis on the arrangement of light and shadow as a fundamental factor in their design. However, this kind of drawing must also be included under the general term of form drawing, which, if we could make up words as easily as do the Germans, we might more properly call *relative-illumination-of-surface-drawing*.

As in the emphasis on calligraphic or ornamental interest in line drawings, in form drawings by Renaissance masters in which the shading is done with the point, a good deal of the final aesthetic value is embodied in the organization of the strokes. In the drawing by Raphael (Plate XXVII) there is a uniformity of spacing and of depth, or a subtle gradation of them, which is a sheer delight. It is something like the controlled spacing — the legato — in a "run" on the piano executed by a master performer. Without this controlled order the result in either instance is likely to seem confused or "muddy."

Abstract Form Drawing

In many drawings by Tiepolo only the broad distinction between directly illuminated and unilluminated surfaces is shown. This might be referred to as abstract form drawing in two values — the tone of the paper for the light, the tone of the bistre wash for the shadow, without transitional tones. Occasionally Tiepolo would drag his brush to suggest soft edges of shadow on the large rounded surfaces, or he might add extra accents of dark to make a three-value instead of a two-value drawing, but in any case the fundamental conception of the drawing is an arbitrarily abstract distinction between what is on the whole in light and that which is on the whole in shadow.

The principle of such abstract drawing might be indicated in diagrammatic form as shown in fig. 38. With the whole range of illumination from light to dark in a given subject represented by the

line A–B, we may let the white of the paper represent everything higher
in value than any arbitrary point C, while we use a tone of gray or
brown, or even black, as in a woodcut, to represent everything darker
than C. We generalize or abstract all the lights and half-lights into a
single tone of light, and all degrees of shadow into a single tone of
dark (Plate XXVIII). We may abstract into three values if we like, as
in fig. 39, or into four or five; but usually a drawing that gets beyond
three or four values tends toward an indication of complete modeling
with many transitional tones.

If the paper should be dark instead of white, this might be used for

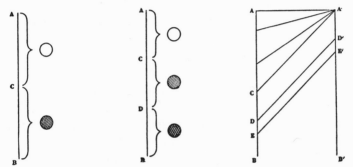

FIG. 38. Form Drawing — Abstraction into Two Values.

FIG. 39. Form Drawing — Abstraction into Three Values.

FIG. 40. Color-Value Drawing on Principle of Sliding Scale.

the shadow, and Chinese white or white chalk used for the light; or the
paper may be used for the half tone in a three-value drawing with
white used for the light and a darker chalk or wash for the shadows.
Many drawings of the Renaissance seem to have been conceived in this
way as primarily renderings in three values; but the lights and darks
are often hatched on in such a manner as to suggest transitional tones
as well, especially on the larger rounded surfaces. This is shown in the
drawing by Filippo Lippi (Plate XXIX).

A two-value drawing will usually suggest an effect of sunlight
because in sunlight the contrast between the light and dark is apt to
be strong and the shadows sharp-edged.

This will suffice to indicate some of the principal types within the
general mode of form drawing. The possibilities of variation are
almost endless. The range of values may be large or small according to

the purpose of the particular drawing and according to the particular medium of silver point, pencil, chalk, ink, or wash, and the tone of the paper employed. In an engraving or drawing with a pointed instrument the lines used in mass to indicate different values may be drawn in such a way as to follow the curving of the various surfaces and so express something of the form by their shape and direction, as in much of Dürer's engraving; or the lines may be hatched in almost regardless of the form of the different surfaces merely to give the required value, as in most of Rembrandt's etchings. In these it will be noticed that there is often no attempt to use shading to express modeling in the lighter passages; the form in the light is given by straight delineation, while modeling in different planes of shadow is indicated by lines which are significant only as they express masses of tone by hatching and cross hatching (Plate XXX). This is a natural way to use either etching or pen-and-ink technique, for ink lines placed far enough apart to render a light tone are apt to appear scratchy. The combination of delineation in lights, kept very broad, with modeling in the shadows, is a large part of the secret of Rembrandt's use of the pure etching technique.[6]

Partial expression of color-value may be employed in a drawing which is mainly in the mode of form drawing, as is explained in the next section; but the mixture of the two modes is likely to be obscure in meaning unless the introduction of color-value is kept very systematic. Many drawings which strike us as rather cheap or commonplace in style often sacrifice real organization and clarity of expression for a superficial prettiness of effect obtained by the introduction of spots of color-value in the midst of what is primarily form drawing.

COLOR-VALUE DRAWING

In color-value drawing, as has already been explained, there is a rendering of the complete visual effect so far as this can be achieved in different values of neutral or monochromatic tones. Examples are to be found in the reproductive engravings after paintings made in the seventeenth, eighteenth, and nineteenth centuries. In these the

[6] A superb example is to be seen in the rare first state of Rembrandt's etching, "The Three Crosses."

aim was to reproduce as far as possible the effect of the original paintings in the terms of black and white and intermediate grays. The engraving by Nanteuil after a portrait by Le Brun is a good example (Plate XXXI). Here the different values of the local tones of whitish fur, flesh, hair, cap, cape, are all clearly distinguished, and they are modeled down toward a possible black with the proper proportion between the different local tones maintained in the different planes of light and shadow. Good examples are to be found in the English mezzotint engravings of the eighteenth and nineteenth centuries made after the portrait paintings of the English masters, and in many of the wood engravings after the old masters by the Americans, Cole and Wolfe. Examples of the same kind of thing in landscape are to be seen in the line engravings after paintings by Turner and other English landscape painters of the early nineteenth century. In order to obtain more of the actual emotional effect achieved in the original designs partly by hue and intensity contrasts, the engravers frequently altered the actual value relations of the painting, substituting value contrasts for hue and intensity contrasts where the composition seemed to demand it. Sometimes this was managed in a reasonable way, but at other times the sharpening up of value contrasts was overdone, so that it spoiled the general effect of the composition.

As has been said above, the photograph and the photo-mechanical engraving processes have superseded reproductive engraving of this sort. A photograph is a rendering in the mode of color-value drawing; but on account of the varying sensitivity of the plate or film to long and short wave lengths, a photograph, even with the use of color filters, rarely approaches absolute accuracy. This is true in the case of photographs of paintings, and students of painting have to be constantly on their guard not to trust too much to the recording of value relations in photographic reproductions.

More recent examples of the color-value mode are to be seen in the ordinary illustrators' wash drawings made for reproduction in half tone. These have been popular in that the reproductions suggest a rather complete pictorial effect; however, most of the best illustrations of recent as well as of earlier times have been done in more limited and more economical modes.

Combination of Form and Color-Value Drawing on Principle of Sliding Scale

Naturally a drawing completely carried out in color-value is easily readable and understandable. As has been suggested in the last section, an equal readability and as satisfactory an indication of the important value contrasts in a subject may be achieved without making an elaborately complete color-value drawing. This perfectly systematic way of indicating the principal color-value differences in a subject may be thought of as a mixture of form drawing and color-value drawing on what might be called a sliding-scale principle. Many examples of this type of drawing have been produced in the last two or three hundred years, as for instance some of the portrait drawings by Van Dyck and many by Ingres and Degas. It is a very natural way for anyone to draw when he feels that he wants to express a little more of the way in which some of the principal value contrasts in a subject attract the eye than is possible in a pure form drawing. Good artists have done this sort of thing so instinctively that it may seem rather foolish to talk about it; but a consistent use of this manner of drawing is particularly difficult, requiring a very keen sense of the relative importance of things, and some explanation may be of use in connection with criticism as well as practice.

Let us suppose that in drawing a portrait we should decide that the contrasts between the values of the objects on the whole fairly light in tone do not interest us very much — between flesh and collar and coat, for example — but that the contrasts made by the darker value of the eyebrow against the flesh, of the hair against the cheek, and by the dark of the pupil of the eye and the dark of the necktie compared with surrounding tones, play an important part in connection with the general character of the subject, and that we want to give some idea of the way in which the eye is attracted by the contrasts made by these darks with adjacent tones. If we were to render all the lighter local tones, perhaps down to middle value, merely in the white of the paper, and then suddenly to put hair and necktie in their true values in relation to white and black, these spots would jump out altogether too strongly. If, instead, we slide up all the values proportionately, as indicated in fig. 40, we may have a perfectly accurate and readable rendering of the relative contrasts of these darker tones as compared with the lighter tones. All values of local tones down as far as what arbitrary point we choose to take, say C, we will transpose into the white of the paper in the plane of light, and model down according to the dark of the particular medium we may be using; all tones below C we will render by values indicated by the diagonal lines drawn parallel to the line C–A′, where they meet the line A′–B′. This seems like a very elaborate explanation for an obvious and simple method of drawing, as in the example by Van Dyck shown in Plate XXXII, but I am convinced that there is a great deal of muddle-headed thinking, resulting in unsatisfactory work, due to a mixing of the modes of form drawing and color-value drawing in an unsystematic fashion. Of course no absolute rule of procedure can be laid down, for a good draftsman may do anything that he finds convenient to express what he thinks of importance. In sketches made as notes for paintings all manner of mixtures of modes will often be found according to the purpose of the artist; but in such drawings it doesn't matter if much is difficult for the ordinary person to understand so long as the artist can understand them himself, and often it is the direct shorthand method of putting things down, regardless of superficial effect, that gives such drawings their interest and charm. Common sense and judgment are required in the use of distinct modes or in combining them.

The sliding-scale method is found particularly in sketch drawings made as studies for paintings, and these are rarely finished drawings. Those by Ingres are usually only sketched in in line in what are considered the less important passages, and finished up in the heads by means of a partial rendering of color-values on the sliding-scale principle. An interesting example by Degas is shown in Plate XXXIII.

6

THE MODES OF PAINTING

The modes of painting may be roughly classified as *mode of line and local tone*; *mode of relief*; *Venetian* or *later Renaissance pictorial mode*; and *the mode of the total visual effect* to which might be added a *hybrid mode* which exhibits a mixture of the points of view of the first two or three modes. This is a very rough classification, and each mode embraces a great many variations. Still, as in the case of drawing considered in the preceding chapter, it is better in many ways not to make too minute a classification; for if a person can get to understand typical examples of these main modes, he will have little difficulty in understanding the variations, or possibly the blending of different modes; and it is well to remember that, after all, such classifications are all more or less arbitrary and are of value only so far as they are useful in increasing our understanding and our power of discrimination of artistic performance. In the present instance, therefore, I shall limit myself to a description of the typical use of each of these four modes and to brief references to possible variations.

After what has been written in a preceding chapter on the general principles governing the appearance of things in nature, there will be little difficulty in understanding what is meant by the mode of the total visual effect. But, as has been said before, there are other ways of painting — that is, of expressing ideas about objects in the terms of painting — which have little to do with the rendering of the actual appearance of things. In most Asiatic painting, for example, no attention is paid to the variations in tone produced by the effect of light and shadow. The idea of rendering the superficial effect of nature probably never occurred to Eastern painters as a reasonable aim. And indeed much may be said for their point of view; for after looking at fine Chinese paintings one is always at first shocked by the apparent triviality of most modern Western art — it often takes some time to recognize that, after all, there is some validity in our interest in atmosphere and light. Similar theoretical and practical justification may be found for the use of other abstract modes; when properly used they possess decided advantages of their own — advantages which are as a rule particularly appropriate to the circumstances under which they were developed.

There is another consideration which should be taken into account. Chinese and most other Asiatic artists [1] seem always most naturally to have expressed form in terms of line while Western artists from the fifth century B.C. in Greece down to the present day have tended to emphasize plastic modeling of surfaces. This is seen even in sculpture if one compares the Chinese figure in Plate XXXIV with the Greek head from Chios dating from the fourth century B.C. (Plate XXXV). In the Chinese figure there is to be sure some rounding out of the main masses but the more detailed cutting of the stone is done to bring out the lines formed by the edges where the different planes meet rather than to give significance to the intermediate surfaces, and one reads the final result as a kind of three-dimensioned delineation. On the other hand, in the Greek head the edges are suppressed and attention is focused on the subtle modeling of surfaces brought out to the observer by the variation in light and shade. The Greek head is an extreme example but it expresses a general tendency and a general point of view.

The plastic point of view prevailed in the West down through Greco-Roman times and its influence hardly ever disappeared completely in Western art. However, just as in all provincial painting based on a plastic tradition there is a tendency to revert to linear expression,[2] so in later classical art there was a gradual breaking down of the plastic tradition and a natural resort to line. Consequently when the Byzantine style in eastern Europe and the Romanesque style in the West finally emerged, expression of form was mainly linear and this is true of sculpture as well as of painting. For example the technique employed by the sculptor of the Moissac tympanum (Plate XXXVI) is surpris-

[1] A possible exception might be noted in the case of earlier Indian artists. The question of the extent of Western influence would have to be considered.

[2] This is to be observed in much of the work of the so-called American "primitives"; these are provincial rather than primitive. The tendency is also constantly to be seen in the work of beginners and of many amateurs.

ingly like that of the Chinese sculptor of the Lung Men figure (Plate XXXIV). We read the form largely by means of the lines made by the edges and the modeling of surface is relatively insignificant. In Byzantine and Romanesque mosaic and painting we find the same emphasis on linear expression. But at the same time, and this is an important point, the derivation from a plastic tradition is always in evidence; except that the variations in light and shadow are often transformed into a pattern that has principal significance in the tonal design rather than as readable modeling of surface. This is seen in the mosaic from San Vitale (Plate XXXVII), and in the Spanish painting (Plate XXXVIII). The derivation from a plastic tradition is often seen even in the way in which line is used: this is to be observed in Byzantine mosaics of the eleventh century like those from Daphni, and is particularly striking in line drawings like those of the Winchester manuscripts, where the sequences emphasized in the drawing of drapery are quite different from those in a Greek vase painting or a Chinese drawing or painting and are to be accounted for only on the supposition of a more or less sketchy technique derived from a plastic manner of drawing.[3]

It is because there is in Byzantine and Romanesque painting a curious mixture of the linear point of view with a disintegrated plastic tradition that the term *hybrid mode* may be applied to it. It is essentially, in its conception, line and local tone but with a trace also of the point of view of the mode of relief.

Modeling with plastic significance was gradually revived in Gothic sculpture and painting and it of course became a dominant feature of Renaissance art. From the Renaissance down to the end of the nineteenth century there have been, as already noted, lapses into an emphasis on line in the work of provincial artists, but, in spite of the greater complexities of all this painting due to the introduction in the sixteenth and seventeenth century of what may be described as a more pictorial point of view, still expression of form remained on the whole in the plastic tradition.

Toward the end of the nineteenth century and in the twentieth century in the work of many of the more adventurous artists, there has been again a breaking down of the plastic tradition into once more a hybrid mode. Here again evidences of modeling have usually not

[3] See Appendix IV.

entirely disappeared, but the variations in tone serve simply to emphasize the linear expression or they become of significance only as part
of the tonal design.

Further discussion of this hybrid mode will appear as we proceed.

MODE OF LINE AND LOCAL TONE

In the mode of representation which we may designate by the name
of *line and local tone*, exemplified particularly in Chinese and other
Asiatic painting, the form is expressed mainly by line, with which
alone, as we have seen in the discussion of delineation above, a surprising amount even of solid form may be shown; but the local tone of
each object is also given by means of pigment spread over its field in
the painting. This is ordinarily flat in each field; but there may be
variation or gradation if, as in the petal of a flower or the wing of a
bird, the local tone is itself varied or graded. Moreover, arbitrary
gradation may be used in order to accent edges and thus assist the
expression of form by the lines. This emphasis by darkening or lighten-
ing the tone to bring out different planes within a field will be found
in the rendering of draperies in a good deal of Chinese painting, as in
some of those of the Sung epoch in the Museum of Fine Arts in Boston — the roll attributed to Hui Tsung (Plate XXXIX), for instance.
It will be found also in some of the full-front Chinese portraits, as in
one in the Fogg Museum (Plate XL), where it is used to bring out the
planes around the nose and the eyes. This has nothing to do with light
and shadow; it is merely a way of distinguishing planes forward and
back, and is perfectly abstract.[4] This general device is used also in
landscape compositions rendered simply in ink (Plate X).

[4] Occasionally one finds examples of earlier Chinese painting in which there
seems to be an approach to actual modeling of surface in a plastic manner. A painting from the Stein collection in the British Museum reproduced in Waley's
Introduction to the Study of Chinese Painting (Plate XXI) suggests an attempt at
such modeling. It may be that the painter had seen examples of this in Indian
prototypes and had modeling definitely in mind, but in reality the result is hardly
more than an abstract distinction of plane such as is described above. Sometimes
lines representing folds of drapery were accented by gradations of tone similar to
the way in which edges were accented in sculpture by a hollowing out of the
surface between the edges. In certain early wall paintings at Tun Huang in
Western China there are traces of lighter tones like crudely executed high lights.
These suggest that the paintings may represent a breaking down of the more plastic

As this mode is completely abstract, it is natural that there should seldom be any attempt to render the tones of a subject in a complete or literal fashion. Unless accessory objects are necessary as a setting for figures, the background may be left perfectly flat; or what objects that are relevant may be shown without any feeling that the whole space of the picture has somehow to be filled up, as in our more realistic style. To a large extent it is felt that the main function of the tone or color is to add interest to the painting, especially from the standpoint of design. Chinese paintings are as a matter of fact often fairly naturalistic in the rendering of the tone of individual objects; but in Persian paintings, executed in the same general mode, rocks are made violet, or pink, or blue, as well as a more natural gray, according to exigencies of tone design, without any regard for actual effect; for the painting is primarily illumination of the surface of the page.

The Chinese painter aimed to express as far as possible the essential character of his subject without regard to superficial effect; in fact he seemed to realize that there were certain essential facts that could be expressed only in completely arbitrary fashion. He therefore constantly transposed the detail of natural forms into abstract line motives, which to be sure occasionally lose something of the variety and mystery of nature, but, in compensation, give the essential organization of structure, or of rhythmical movement, with a clearness and force not possible by any other means. Thus, as has been pointed out in connection with line drawing, flame, cloud, running water, curling wave and foam, folds of drapery, are all interpreted by line motives or by broader strokes of the brush which could be learned almost as so much calligraphy (Plate XLI). Indeed the different strokes employed to represent natural forms were taught by master to pupil as a vocabulary, and they were practiced over and over, like strokes used in writing, until an almost inconceivable subtlety and dexterity as well as expressiveness of touch were achieved. Moreover, as has also been noted

style of Indian painting from which Chinese Buddhist art was derived. As much of the plastic quality in Indian art derived from Greek art by way of Gandhara, this actually parallels the breaking down of the plastic tradition of classical art in Byzantine and Romanesque painting. In some examples of Chinese and Japanese painting there is practically no delineation, and the mode becomes one simply of juxtaposed areas of local tone. In many details of Indian wall painting, like that at Ajanta, in which more important figures or objects show modeling in relief, there is a similar rendering of local tones without delineation.

above, Chinese and Japanese painters constantly thought of the emotional effect produced by different kinds of strokes, and often achieved mystical or dramatic expression in this abstract manner; and they also considered the significance, from the standpoint of formal design, of the repetition of the same general shape of stroke throughout a composition.

It will be seen, therefore, that when it comes to the expression of certain kinds of ideas, there are definite advantages in the mode of line and local tone, as compared with more naturalistic modes. It lent itself peculiarly well to the expression of the mystical spirit of Chinese Buddhism, and to the poetic treatment of nature found in Chinese and Japanese landscape painting. It was admirably adapted also to the decorative style developed by the Japanese, while, with certain modifications, it lent itself perfectly to the representation of extremely realistic figure subjects by later so-called popular masters, like Hokusai.

Perspective projection may be used in this mode, but ordinarily it has not been employed. Chinese and Japanese painters regularly used the method of diagonal projection, or something approaching it. In Egyptian painting geometric projection, or some variation of it, resulting in what may be called "profile drawing" of individual objects, is to be found. Similar profile drawing, but often with greater naturalism in the rendering of the figure, was used in Greek painting.

This same mode was also employed in most Persian painting, in Rajput painting in India, and also in Egyptian and earlier Greek painting — the latter at its best unfortunately only partially revealed to us in the work of the Greek vase painters. There are also examples of medieval painting and stained glass which to all intents and purposes are in this mode, although they are seldom perfect instances. As pointed out above most of the earlier medieval painting, as well as a large part of Byzantine, may be regarded as hybrid in mode, in that it combined the main "line and local tone" principles of Oriental painting with the plastic traditions of later Greek and Roman art.

Considerable use has also been made of the mode of line and local tone by painters of our own day who have experimented with this as with other abstract modes. Interesting examples are to be found in the work of Van Gogh, Gauguin, Matisse, and Picasso, but usually with a mixing in of a bit of plastic or pictorial suggestion in a hybrid manner.

MODE OF RELIEF

General Character — Its Use in Medieval and Renaissance Italian Painting

In the mode of relief, as the name implies, emphasis is placed on the plastic modeling of surface, and so naturally the most typical examples are found in Italian paintings of the developed Renaissance of the fifteenth century and of the early sixteenth century. However at the beginning of the fourteenth century the still Gothic Giotto marks the real beginning of the more definite use of this mode with his emphasis on the expression of solid form by modeling of surface, as opposed to the more linear Byzantine manner which still prevailed in the work of Duccio.[5]

One of the most clear-cut examples of the mode of relief is to be found in the "Last Supper" painted by Andrea del Castagno in the refectory of S. Apollonia in Florence in the second half of the fifteenth century (Plate XLII). In this there is a representation of the solid form of the figures and draperies by a rendering of modeling in light and shade; but, except for the use of perspective, there is hardly any closer approach than in Chinese painting to a suggestion of the superficial appearance of things in nature. The figures are seated in a long room with the light apparently admitted through a window which is seen at the right. But in the painting the light is made to fall on the wall and on the figures far removed from this window with the same force as on the wall and figures near the window; and, although the drapery over the knees of each figure is obviously placed under the table, and so naturally in the dark, the form of this part of the drapery is rendered with exactly the same set of lights, half-lights, and shadows as that above the table. Moreover no shadow is cast by any figure upon the one adjoining; each one is firmly modeled in full range of light and

[5] "This Giotto changed the art of painting from the Greek to the Latin [manner], and brought it to the modern [style]" (*The Book of the Art of Cennino Cennini*, translated by Christiana J. Herringham, London, 1899). Giotto was no doubt influenced by the sculptors who in turn were emulating the plastic expression of ancient Roman art.

shade. For this particular picture this is perfectly right, for the monumental decorative effect of the composition would have been ruined
if any naturalistic effect of light had been introduced.

A comparison with a relief by Donatello will show that the aim of
the painter was practically the same as that of the sculptor — to represent the solid form of each figure in plastic fashion, but to give no more
effect of atmospheric envelope than may be given in sculpture by
higher and lower relief. Comparison of a painting by Giotto with a
relief by Andrea Pisano (Plates XLIII and XLIV) or one by Benozzo
Gozzoli with a relief by Ghiberti illustrates this perfectly clearly
(Plates XLV and XLVI). In the painting by Benozzo a few indications
of cast shadow will be found, but they are purely incidental remarks
and have nothing to do with the main effect or with the general conception of the work. Whereas the Chinese painter, and sculptor too for
that matter, thought to express form principally by line, the painter
of the fourteenth or fifteenth century in Italy followed his contemporary sculptors in aiming to express form principally by plastic
modeling of surface.

At the same time the local tones of the different fields were given,
and usually more completely and realistically than in Asiatic painting.
There was, however, never any complete regard for natural relations
of values and intensities in the different planes of modeling. In the
typical painting of the fourteenth century and of the earlier part of the
fifteenth century, as in most of the works of Fra Angelico for example,
the different values in each field were ordinarily obtained by mixing a
colored pigment with white pigment. This would mean in the case of a
red drapery that the highest intensity would come in the plane of the
shadow, and the lowest intensity in the plane of light, as shown in
fig. 41. This is of course the reverse of the natural sequence. Sometimes
yellow would be used instead of white, in which case a drapery might
be red in the plane of shadow, orange in the plane of half-light, and
yellow or orange-yellow in the plane of light; or a green drapery
might be modeled from green in shadow to yellow-green or yellow in
the light; or a blue or blue-violet might be carried through green-blue
to green or yellow-green in the light — the range of hues, like the
range of values, would depend on circumstances.[6] This gave less differ-

[6] The same sequences toward yellow in the light are found in Byzantine

ence between the intensity in light and that in shadow, and often suggested a yellowish general tonality to harmonize with the gold of the background; but it was not usually carried out very consistently. One field might be modeled up toward yellow while one adjacent was modeled toward white, or possibly in a less obviously ordered sequence like some described by Cennino Cennini. Red mixed with white paint was apt to give a slight swing toward violet in the light and this was sometimes emphasized with the addition of blue. Some fields were even modeled toward black in the shadow. The dark blue of the Madonna's robe was constantly treated in this way to distinguish it from lighter blues worn perhaps by angels. Flesh tone usually depended on a play

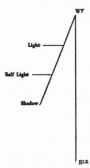

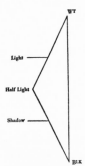

Fig. 41. The Modeling of a Red Drapery with the Highest Intensity in the Shadow.

Fig. 42. The Modeling of a Red Drapery with the Highest Intensity in the Half-Light.

of red and green, obtained by painting in different values of red over a ground tone of *verde terra*. The particular way in which any individual field was modeled would depend largely on exigencies of expression and of design — the relation of each field to those surrounding and to the composition as a whole. It was largely a problem in the relative attraction of the different tones in the composition.[7] The range

mosaics, and in Gothic and Renaissance tapestries, mixed in with the use of a single hue in different values. Prescriptions for these different ways of modeling a drapery are given by Cennino Cennini (*op. cit.*).

[7] The particular method of painting varied considerably. In larger fields both in tempera and fresco three main tones were usually mixed in separate jars or pots. Then the darks, half-lights, and lights were applied each in its own part of the whole field and only finally joined together to form a transition from plane to plane of modeling. Each tone meant a distinct plane of modeling like a sculptured plane in stone or bronze. High lights and deep darks were added as accents. In

of values in each field would ordinarily depend on the amount of contrast desired in the particular field. The "placing" of a given field forward or back was often controlled by the range of tone in this field compared with that in other fields. No attention was paid to the proportional diminution of contrasts found in nature as objects model from light into shadow. In fig. 33 in Chapter IV we saw that in nature under uniform conditions the range of light and dark in the modeling of a white drapery would be greater than in the modeling of a dark blue drapery. But in painting in the mode of relief as practiced in the Middle Ages and the Renaissance it would depend entirely on individual circumstances of design and expression whether the wider range of values would come in the blue or in the white.

In much fourteenth-century painting, figures and objects were thought of as so many flat silhouettes that could be arranged on the flat surface of the panel or the wall to make a satisfactory decorative composition. In altarpieces like that by Spinello Aretino shown in Plate XLVII there was a constant tendency to subordinate expression of form to decorative effect. The modeling in different values with possibly a sequence of color in the different planes seemed necessary to give sufficient tonal interest to the fields in which plain stuffs were indicated; but in the painting of gold brocades there would often be no attempt to model out the plastic form, since the flat pattern gave all the interest that was necessary in these fields. The existence of figures forward and back was hardly considered. Until the fifteenth century it was only an occasional painter, like Giotto, who conceived of his figures as in any way occupying space in three dimensions.

In other cases, especially in the fifteenth century, the result was often not so far removed from natural effect as one might at first suppose. The painters of the Renaissance came to employ much greater subtlety than earlier painters in the play of warm and cool grays, and in general in the use of tones obtained by the blending of different pigments. Moreover, partly on account of certain changes in

---

smaller fields, especially those in the miniature illumination of manuscripts (see translation of *Liber de Coloribus Illuminatorum Sine Pictorum*, from Sloane MS. no. 1754, by Daniel V. Thompson, Jr.; *Speculum*, Vol. I, No. 3, July, 1926), and sometimes also in larger fields in tempera painting and even in fresco, a flat middle tone was often applied over the whole field and the lights and darks added on top of this.

technical procedure, shadows were often made lower in intensity than the half-light or light, so that very frequently there resulted a suggestion of broadly diffused light effect. When objects in nature are seen in broadly diffused light, as in the case of figures seen out-of-doors with the sun veiled by thin cloud, one thinks first of the different local tones within each field of which there is only slight variation of value; the modeling in each field is of secondary importance and cast shadows are hardly noticeable. The deeper folds of drapery go down slightly toward black, with some areas of greater intensity, no doubt, on account of reflected light within the folds, while the lights reflect something of the whitish tone of the sky, and so are neutralized slightly. The predominating tone in each field becomes a sort of half-light, with small areas of somewhat neutralized lights and shadows, which, in relation to the general effect, play a comparatively minor part. The modeling of a red field under such circumstances might be something like that in fig. 42.[8] A suggestion of this effect of diffused light is often found in the frescoes of the fifteenth century. A good example in tempera painting is to be seen in the "Annunciation," attributed to Antoniazzo Romano, in the Gardner Museum in Fenway Court (Plate XLVIII). The frescoes of Piero della Francesca in Arezzo may be cited as other examples.

Toward the end of the fifteenth century Italian painters (even other than those directly under Flemish influence) began to experiment with the representation of cast shadows, but these experiments were almost always confined to incidental details or small passages in the background. Some instances are found in the work of Piero della Francesca, others in the paintings of the San Bernardino series in Perugia attributed to various masters, a suggestion in Domenico Veneziano's altarpiece in the Uffizi in Florence. These experiments, however, did not alter the character of the representation as a whole.

In the landscape backgrounds there is often considerable effect of space and even of atmosphere. This was achieved by very simple means and in such a way that the landscape still harmonized with the abstract rendering of the foreground. In the work of Giotto and of other masters of the fourteenth century, as in the relief sculpture

[8] Sometimes the paint itself when applied more thickly in the darks tends to absorb more light and thus to produce a lowering of intensity.

of the same time, landscape detail was modeled in relief with almost the same force as the figures; there was no attempt to render space in painting any more than in sculpture. In the fifteenth century, as an understanding of diminution of size in perspective came to be understood, and sculptors developed the technique of representing different planes forward and back by higher and lower relief, the painters followed suit and showed different planes of architecture and landscape in precisely the same manner as in sculpture in relief; the modeling in lower and lower relief suggested the diminution of contrasts with greater and greater distance. Then, possibly influenced by Flemish painting, where this had been done earlier, painters hit on the scheme of grading the sky down toward a pale gray at the horizon and of setting the shapes of blue hills against this sky, gradually giving a little more contrast and a little more variety of tone toward the foreground. In the landscape distance this amounted usually to little more than a play of neutralized oranges and blues — of relative warm and cool tones. The result was almost always a suggestion of early morning before sunrise — a clear atmosphere with the main source of light in the sky above the horizon, and the hills paler and paler blue in the distance against this warm sky. The effect of light in this had nothing to do with the illumination of the figures in the foreground. But it didn't matter. The form of the figures was most easily studied in the side lighting of the studio; the landscape was most naturally represented in early morning light. After all, the whole thing was only conventional expression of visual concepts. As long as this was understandable and harmonious, it never occurred to these Renaissance painters to bother about mere literalness. Painting was an expression of visual concepts, not simply a matter of momentary appearance.

The phenomenon of diminution of size with distance was observed by painters in Italy by the middle of the fourteenth century as by northern painters at about the same time. There was evidently also some realization of the fact that parallel lines appear to converge on a point; but the rendering of this was haphazard and appeared alongside of "diagonal projection" often in the same picture. By the middle of the fifteenth century there was systematic study of the laws of perspective, and from then on perspective projection was employed. Until some two or more centuries later, however, this was mostly confined to parallel or "one point" perspective (that is, where rectangular objects have two sides parallel to the picture plane). It must be noted also that painters seldom allowed scientific accuracy to get in the way of reasonable expression of idea; so they disregarded literal perspective when they saw fit. Within approximately single planes they sometimes disregarded the matter of diminution of size with distance. Foreshortening they thought of as more or less independent of perspective, as is illustrated in the famous "Dead Christ," by Mantegna in the Brera in Milan (Plate XLIX), where the figure is shown lying on the ground, feet foremost, without any perspective diminution to reduce the size of the head and shoulders.

In all this painting the mode of representation was closely related to the technical procedures employed. Fresco, in which the pigment was mixed simply with water and applied to a wall surface on sections of wet plaster from day to day, and tempera, in which the pigment was mixed with yolk of egg and applied to a dry white ground of *gesso* (whiting or gypsum and glue) spread over a wooden panel, both required very systematic procedures and definite formulas for the handling of individual fields. They lent themselves particularly well to expression in the mode of relief and to the achievement of a monumental decorative effect which was the dominant aim of the painters.

Painting in the mode of relief was probably first practiced in Greece in the early part of the fourth century, or even in the last of the fifth century, before Christ. Parrhasios is said to have been the first painter to experiment with the idea of light and shade, but it was only natural that the Greek painters should have desired to adopt the method of plastic modeling developed by the sculptors in the fifth century. As a matter of fact we know little about Greek painting of the fifth and fourth centuries, since there are no extant examples of any importance, and we are reduced to conjecture on the basis of descriptions by ancient authors. We do know, however, that if there had been at first a natural use of some kind of relief mode, it was soon replaced by a more pictorial mode — closely approaching that of sixteenth-century Venice — as we see it in the paintings of Pompeii and Herculaneum and a few other examples, though most of this is in the nature of provincial house-decorator's work.

The breaking down of the classical plastic and pictorial tradition into a hybrid style or mode may be seen in the paintings and mosaics of the fourth, fifth, and sixth centuries after Christ. In the portrait head from the Fayum in Egypt (Plate L) the light and shade formulas were reduced pretty much to a linear pattern, and this is seen also in mosaics like those in the tomb of Galla Placidia in Ravenna of the fifth century and those in San Vitale of the sixth century. Linear or rather flattish light and dark patterns are seen throughout Byzantine and Romanesque art. And yet there was some modeling of surface especially in the faces, and in the tenth- and eleventh-century Byzantine mosaics sometimes it was very subtle. At any rate the modeling in light and shade in the mode of relief in later Medieval and in Renaissance painting was based on the survival of at least a vestige of the plastic idea in Byzantine art.

With the more naturalistic tendencies introduced in Gothic times, the variations in light and shade were given more significance from the point of view of plastic expression. Thus, as has already been suggested, there was close similarity between the practice of Giotto and that of sculptors of the same time, and during the fifteenth century the art of sculpture dominated the practice of painting in Italy almost completely. Mantegna, the great master of the Paduan school, and the Venetian painter, Crivelli, in some ways even more (Plates LI and LII), show extreme sculptural tendencies. In Crivelli's painting, as often in that of the fourteenth century, actual modeling of ornamental details in relief and painting in the manner of relief are juxtaposed in the same composition without any suggestion of incongruity.

Like many of the masters of the fifteenth century, Michelangelo was sculptor as well as painter; so in his figure of Adam on the ceiling of the Sistine Chapel (Plate LIII) he seems to have hewn out the forms by means of planes of light, half-light, and shadow, almost as if he had been using chisel and mallet.

Occasional painters or groups of painters inclined toward a more linear mode of representation; and much of the abstract calligraphy that we associate with the art of the East appears in the work of Simone Martini in Siena in the fourteenth century, and in the gay, decorative painting produced all over Europe around the year 1400, a phase of art to which the French writer Courajod has applied the term "international style." Botticelli, at the end of the fifteenth century, seems to have returned consciously to a more linear manner in order better to render his mystical rather than naturalistic conceptions.

Leonardo, on the other hand, developed a sort of hybrid mode all his own in aiming partly at higher relief of modeling, and partly at a striking effect of light, suggested possibly in the first place by the example of Flemish painting.

We see then that, in general, this mode of relief — or we might call it sculptural mode — was one particularly adapted for monumental decoration, harmonizing with the plastic sculptural detail employed in Gothic and early Renaissance architecture and furniture; and it was adapted also for the expression of the early Renaissance interest in the form of the human figure. It was not merely primitive in itself, although many examples might very properly be called so. In the way of monumental decoration it offered distinct advantages over more pictorial modes. It is for this reason that certain modern painters have sought to adopt it, especially in decorative work.

VENETIAN OR LATER RENAISSANCE PICTORIAL MODE

In spite of the variations in its use the general idea of the mode of relief is easily explained and easily understood. But when it comes to the third of our broad classifications the task is not so easy. Sir Charles Holmes has said that in general while "the noblest examples of Italian painting appear to tend toward the condition of a coloured bas-relief . . . the cabinet pictures of Holland tend in the same manner toward the condition of an open window"; [9] in other words, the complete visual effect rendered in completely realistic fashion. Now in between, or perhaps rather beside these two points of view, is another, developed by the Venetian painters of the sixteenth century, and adopted by a great many other painters of the sixteenth, seventeenth, and eighteenth centuries — at least outside of Holland. It is difficult to find an appropriate name for this mode, and I do not know of any that is entirely satisfactory. The mode is more completely pictorial than that of relief employed by painters of the fifteenth century, and yet it is distinct from the realistic mode used by a painter like Vermeer and at least

[9] Sir Charles Holmes, *Old Masters and Modern Art* (London, 1924–1927), II, xxvii–xxviii.

approached by the Van Eycks and their followers as early as the fifteenth century. Because in this mode there is a more complete rendering of effect of light and shadow than in the mode of relief, it might be called *full chiaroscuro*; but the fact that the word *chiaroscuro* (*chiaro* = light; *scuro* = shade) has been used in other senses in connection with Italian painting makes the term somewhat misleading. So it may best be referred to as the *Venetian mode of the sixteenth century*, or simply as *Venetian mode*; or, since it is employed by post-Renaissance painters who follow Venetian precedent, it may be called *later Renaissance pictorial mode*. For the present we may find it convenient to use these terms more or less interchangeably, as long as we understand that we are talking about the same general point of view, or minor modifications of this. As a matter of fact it will be impossible to draw any sharp line between this mode and that of the total visual effect. In many cases it is merely a matter of general aim. Nevertheless in typical examples this mode is easily enough distinguished.

Perhaps the clearest examples are to be found in the work of Titian and Tintoretto. In the painting of "St. Mark and the Slave" by Tintoretto (Plate LIV), for instance, it will be seen that the whole character of the design depends on the throwing of large numbers of the figures into broad masses of shadow, which are relieved against correspondingly broad masses of light. In a similar way in the "Entombment" by Titian (Plate LV) the whole force of the design depends on the placing of the head of the Christ back in a deep mass of shadow, which is relieved against the light of the sky breaking in the distance. This gives a dramatic effect which could not possibly have been achieved in a merely sculpturesque way of painting. It is not at all sculpturesque; it is pictorial. And yet it is a use of pictorial terms in quite a different way from what we find in a painting by Vermeer, or de Hoogh, or Degas. In the latter there is perfectly real daylight and space, and the surface of the picture is to a large extent lost sight of. In the other there is, to be sure, expression of space forward and back, and of large effect of light and shadow, but within conventional limits, and with very little loss of feeling of surface, of architectural significance. When one comes to examine Venetian painting closely, one finds that the rendering of space is in fact accomplished largely by abstract means, and not by an exact rendering of value and intensity relations, as in a

Vermeer; and that, in spite of the general effect of large masses of light and shadow, the tone relations in individual fields depend more on exigencies of pigment material and technical procedures and design than on any attempt at accurate naturalistic rendering of tone relations.

The "Rape of Europa" (Plate LVI), one of Titian's later works, now in Fenway Court in Boston, may be taken as a typical example for the abstract expression of space. It has always seemed to me that in its method of expression this painting actually approaches more closely to Chinese painting than to most modern European painting. Chinese painters in ink achieve an expression of planes forward and back by a suppression of detail or of contrast in a distant plane in order to snap out the edge of a nearer object perfectly clearly; the rendering of detail is always subordinated to this more important matter of plane. In the painting of the dragon by Ch'ên Jung (Plate LVII), for example, the details of scales on the neck are suppressed where they might conflict with the nearer mass of the head, the details of which are strongly accented in light; but the scales are shown more clearly farther along where it is necessary to show this particular bit of the corkscrew curve of the neck in front of the farther part. The sense of planes here is very definite, and one might at first almost be inclined to think that the Chinese painter was trying to suggest light and shadow; but a careful study of this and a comparison with other examples will show that it is a matter of relative contrast to separate the planes, and not at all a question of light and shadow. In this particular case the suppression of detail runs toward an even tone of dark; but in most landscape painting the suppression is the other way, toward the light ground of the silk or the paper. The general principle involved in this is the same as in the case of expression of planes forward and back in delineation, as explained in the preceding chapter; it is a matter of marking the disconnections between different planes, and of suppressing contrasts in the more distant planes.

If we turn now to the "Europa," we find almost exactly the same device made use of to distinguish the planes in the painting of the head and upraised arm and of the flying scarf and sky beyond. In order to bring out the arm against the scarf, the tone of the scarf where it comes near the arm is reduced until it contrasts only very slightly with the sky; and against these slight contrasts, relatively strong contrasts bring the head and the arm of the figure clearly forward. Where they will no longer interfere with the figure, the contrasts on the scarf are slightly increased so that it will hold its place properly in front of the lesser contrasts of the sky. In a similar way the knee of the "Europa" is "placed" convincingly in air in front of the sky, which is only very subtly modulated, by the exact adjustment of contrasts of light and dark. A somewhat similar and most interesting example of this exact "placing" forward and back is to be found in the hand of the Ariadne, raised beyond the head and against the sky, in Titian's "Bacchus and Ariadne" in the National Gallery in London. Of course this use of light and dark is conceived in such a manner as to harmonize in general with the broad effect of light; but the definition of light effect is approximate, not specific, and it is sacrificed if necessary for the sake of more important matters. This exact "placing" of objects forward and back is one of the principal concerns of the Venetian painter, and it is achieved always by careful adjustment of contrasts, assisted at times by variations in the handling of the paint — sharper crisp touches ordinarily coming forward, and softer touches going back. There is nothing of the exact proportioning of values and intensities like that which accounts for the realistic light and atmosphere in the work of Vermeer. It is truly almost as pure abstraction as in the case of Chinese painting.

In our particular example there is further evidence of the relative non-naturalism of the mode; for without any seeming incongruity Europa and the Bull are shown as if we were down on their level, only two or three feet above the surface of the water, while we look down on the distant shore from a considerable height.[10] Such a playing with actual perspective would seem like inexcusable distortion if the painting were carried out in the "open window" manner of Holland; here it passes unnoticed. It is a "picture," as distinct from a view through an "open window." Besides, it was intended to be a tapestry-like decoration of surface, as in the case of the fifteenth- or fourteenth-century paintings; only here the design depended primarily on the play of masses of light and dark arranged in a more or less arbitrary fashion,

[10] Further evidence of a disregard for mere literal rendering is found if one attempts to analyze the structure of the figure of Europa from a strictly anatomical point of view; and yet the action is completely convincing. After all the main business of the painter is to produce an illusion — an illusion of reality — and this often has little to do with literal likeness.

and all this painting was meant to go with a different style of architecture, in which the heavy gold moldings allowed somewhat greater
freedom in the pictorial arrangement than did the flatter decorative
schemes of the fifteenth century. When painting a portrait, moreover,
the artist did not represent all his accessories as he might actually
see them in reality; he played with their tones perfectly freely, sub-
ordinating contrasts which would interfere with the main scheme of
concentration of interest on the head and figure, and, in general, ad-
justing his tones to consistent expression of character and to satisfactory
design.[11]

This mode, developed in Venice out of the later fifteenth-century
painting which had been based on Flemish work, was adopted elsewhere in Italy in the sixteenth century and over much of the rest of
Europe in the sixteenth and seventeenth centuries. It might be thought
of as the imaginative pictorial mode of the later Renaissance.[12] Aside
from the painting of the sixteenth-century Venetians, or of the
Venetian-trained El Greco, one may cite that of Rubens, of Van
Dyck, of Poussin, of Tiepolo of eighteenth-century Venice, of Fragon-
ard, of Reynolds, of Copley, or Stuart. It is all in this same imaginative
pictorial mode. At the end of the sixteenth and the beginning of the
seventeenth century, a number of painters, especially Caravaggio and
those more or less strongly under his influence — men like Ribera,
Guercino, Rembrandt, and Velásquez in his earlier work — varied the
usual aspect of painting in this general mode by a crowding of the
darks, as explained in a later chapter. But this was merely a variation
within the main general point of view. In all of this painting one will
find to a considerable extent higher intensities and stronger contrasts

---

[11] A good example is to be seen in the portrait of the Earl of Arundel by
Rubens in the Gardner Museum in Boston. Here the sky seen under the arch is
kept extraordinarily low in value, and the details of molding in back of the head
are dropped off an inch or two from the outline of the head so that there may be
no confusion of planes. In portraits by Renaissance and Baroque painters it may
often be observed that the tone of the background is made lighter or darker in a
perfectly arbitrary way to define the outline of the head or of other details in
the foreground. This arbitrary device, often in an exaggerated form, was frequently used by Cézanne.

[12] Here again the mode of expression is definitely related to the technique —
in this case oil painting on canvas, developed by the Venetian painters in the
sixteenth century and varied somewhat by painters of the seventeenth and eighteenth centuries.

in the light and lesser contrasts in the shadow, but not usually on any exact proportional basis; and in this mode it seems not at all incongruous to do anything with the light effect that seems convenient from the standpoint of the design or from the standpoint of expression of subject matter. Moreover the expression of space forward and back is always a matter of more or less abstract and often unnatural adjustment of contrasts and of handling of the paint itself.

MODE OF THE TOTAL VISUAL EFFECT

The difficulty with distinguishing certain examples of this mode from those of the preceding mode lies in the fact that, within appropriate limits, a good deal of the abstract "painter's license" of the latter may be employed in painting in which the aim is really the rendering of the complete visual effect, as for instance in a certain amount of arbitrary suppression of detail to accent the separation of planes forward and back. Nevertheless the typical examples may be distinguished without difficulty, and I must repeat that as long as we understand clearly what the painter is driving at, and how he achieves his results, it doesn't much matter about our classifications, which are merely a means toward understanding and judgment.

The most clear-cut and probably the finest examples of this mode that have been produced are certain of the paintings by Vermeer, the Dutch master who worked in the middle of the seventeenth century. I may refer the reader to the book by Holmes (cited on p. 88) for a discussion of what is appropriate to the "open window" manner of painting adopted by Vermeer, and consider here merely the means with which the result is accomplished. Having adopted the general aims of the Dutch painters of cabinet pictures, Vermeer seems to have had an extraordinary feeling for that proportional relationship of tones, all obedient to a single source of light, which was discussed in the first chapter. This may be felt even in a photograph of the picture from the Czernin collection in Vienna (Plate LVIII), for the photograph shows the subtlety of the value relations fairly accurately. In the picture itself there is a similar subtlety in the rendering of the intensity relations. It is a perfectly simple straightforward rendering of the subject, without exaggeration of any kind; and the feeling for perfectly definite space and clear atmosphere depends chiefly on the refined accuracy with which the tones in the shadows are rendered. It is comparatively easy to define tones in the plane of light, but where most painters go wrong is in the shadow. If the muddy approximations of the darker tones in the work of some of our so-called nineteenth- or twentieth-century "Vermeers" is observed, this will be apparent. In the particular painting by Vermeer referred to, exactly the same relationship, though with lowered value and intensity, is kept between the white of the linen, the red of the stockings, the black of the baggy trousers, in the planes of shadow and deep shadow as in the light. When there is any suggestion of reflection of the outdoor light in a surface, there is likewise just the right degree of neutralization. One characteristic example of Vermeer's subtlety is shown in the painting of the jacket and trousers. The jacket is a cool black, the trousers warm black, and this distinction is not only shown in the light but is kept in the extreme shadow where the actual contrast is almost nothing at all. It is this exactness of relation of value and intensity in the different planes of light that makes the objects "go back" beyond the plane of the picture — to exist in light and space.

This is an entirely different way of expressing existence forward and back from what we find in Venetian painting. It reveals an interest in the organization of tones and in the resulting general harmony as such, entirely distinct from the interest in the mere surface form of individual objects, or the interest in a general pictorial effect. As distinguished from the imaginative figure-subject, or the motive of sculpturesque form, this became the main interest of a painter like Vermeer and to a large extent of many of his contemporaries. It has also been one of the dominant motives in much of the best painting of the nineteenth and twentieth centuries — not merely as a means to the end of dramatic expression or sentimental story-telling, or pleasant picturesqueness, as in so much of the painting that has been produced in the last hundred years, but as a definite end in itself. Such, for instance, are the paintings of simple everyday subjects by Manet and Degas, and especially the still lifes by Monet and Manet. When this interest in the tonal organization in a subject is realized as a definite motive for painting, a still life may become as significant in its way as a figure subject or a landscape.

Actually Vermeer's painting in its most typical examples was not a literal rendering of the optical effect but what might be thought of as a super-realism. Even in the case of an indoor subject like the Czernin Vermeer (Plate LVIII), it is probable that if the eye were adapted to viewing the tones in the more strongly illuminated portion of the room, one could not without a change of adaptation [13] make out the subtle distinctions of tone in the deep dark as precisely as Vermeer renders them. Consequently in Vermeer's painting we have an expression of super-reality, a rendering of a concept which produces an organization of tones beyond what the eye can see — an effect of reality of space and light beyond what one could perceive in looking at the subject itself. Vermeer disregards the optical effect which to the eye adjusted for the lighter portions of the subject produces a certain blankness or indeterminateness in the deeper shadows as actually seen. On the other hand, a painter like Degas, in painting a subject like the "Rehearsal of the Ballet" (Plate LXIV), with figures placed in front of large windows through which the observer is looking to housetops and sky in outdoor light, takes into account the gray blankness with loss of detail on the near side of the figures seen against the light. Degas takes into account the actual momentary optical effect which is entirely ignored by Vermeer, who renders a concept unlike what he actually sees at any one moment. It is a matter of super-realism opposed to optical effect.

Optical effect would seem to be taken slightly into account by Velázquez in "Las Meniñas" and it was taken into account by Rembrandt in some of his later paintings in which the eye seems to be adapted for indoor light so that a passage in strong illumination becomes hardly more than a uniform glare.

Another point to be noted is that in all painting, even in the case of an indoor subject, the range of values in the painting is considerably less than that in the actual subject in which tones of objects turned toward the light are higher than the white of paint on the canvas and the deeper darks are darker than black paint. In a painting the relations of the values may of course be rendered accurately as shown in fig. 43; but in this case there are not as many appreciable distinctions of value in the painting as in the subject, and so some of the distinctions which indicate form and texture in the subject are necessarily lost. This is

[13] See Evans (op. cit.) for a discussion of the principle of adaptation.

precisely what happens in a painting by Vermeer, and it is this which for one thing distinguishes his work from much of that of his contemporaries like Terborch and Metsu. Vermeer deliberately sacrifices the indication of minute texture for the sake of the general organization of tone relations. In much of the painting of other Dutch masters there is what seems a vulgar overinsistence on textures of satins, velvets, and so on at the expense of the general organization and so to some extent at the expense of convincing effect of light and space. To achieve the minute distinctions of value on which the feeling of texture depends the artist extends the value range of individual fields beyond their proportionate relation to the whole value range and thus throws them slightly out of relation to each other. I believe that one finds the same sort of thing in much of the so-called academic painting of the nineteenth century. The painting of the so-called "Impressionists" on the other hand, emphasizes the more accurate rendering of essential *relations* and the consequent suppression of exaggerated rendering of surface textures.

Aside from its problematical use in ancient painting — that is in Greece at the time of Alexander — the mode of the total visual effect found its first real exponent in Jan van Eyck in the fifteenth century. In the portrait of Arnolfini and his wife in the National Gallery in London (Plate LIX), and in some of the small portrait heads, the painting approaches completely that "condition of the open window" which Sir Charles Holmes describes. In the "Arnolfini and his Wife" one finds perhaps for the first time in any extensive subject a consistent proportional diminution of contrasts from light into shadow, and hence a complete realization of space and light, as compared with the use of higher intensities in the shadow, as in all earlier painting, with the consequent suggestion of colored relief or of mere modeling added to a fundamental conception of flat tones. Moreover, in this painting there is a completely realized conception of a light source within the picture; the corners of the room removed from the direct light of the windows are in deep shadow, while the strength of illumination on the wall and floor and on the various objects in the room gradually increases as all these things come more and more into the direct light from out-of-doors. This entirely new conception of the art of painting was probably due in part to the use of the perfected oil or varnish technique which enabled the painters to get subtle distinctions in the deep darks impossible in the tempera or fresco techniques. In this technique, in which the final surface was produced with a rich paint, intensities lower in the darks than in the lights are almost inevitable. This fitted in naturally with the realistic tendencies of the Flemish artists; and the two things, technique and mode, developed together.

In other occasional works of the fifteenth and sixteenth centuries, in portraits especially, as in many by Van der Weyden and by Memlinc, and by Antonello da Messina and other Venetians of the fifteenth century — practically all following the primary lead of Van Eyck — one also finds almost completely consistent rendering of the visual effect. The small "St. Jerome" by Antonello da Messina (Plate LX), in the National Gallery in London, is a striking example of an indoor subject; and the "St. Sebastian" in the Dresden Gallery, also by Antonello (Plate LXI), is a most unusual rendering of outdoor light effect, with the sharp-edged shadows of real sunlight, to have been produced before the seventeenth century.

In other Flemish painting, as indeed in most other northern painting of the fifteenth century, there was a tendency to model down in each field toward lower intensities in the shadow; but there was usually little attempt to be completely realistic in the treatment of light effect. For instance, cast shadows were left out, as in Van Eyck's small triptych in Dresden (Plate LXII), wherever they would have been in the way in the general design. In this case they would have spoiled the monumental effect desired in the composition as a whole. In landscape early morning effect was usually represented, independent of the regular studio lighting of the foreground (Plate LXIII).[14] In many composi-

[14] This combination of one kind of light in the foreground with another kind in the landscape background, which has been noted in Italian as well as Flemish painting of the fifteenth century, is an example of the general rationalization of all this painting. After all if one sits in a room where one can by one adaptation of the eye see objects in the room and by another adaptation can look out of a window and see a distant mountainous landscape, one's concept is not confined to what one sees at either moment by itself, but is a combination of the two. A painting in the manner of Van Eyck would be a truer record of one's memory — of one's concept — than a painting in the manner of a nineteenth-century impressionist.

The other day a friend of mine showed me some photographs of his country house in New Hampshire. Some of these were of rooms in the house with views

tions it is only in details that one finds occasional bits of completely realistic lighting. Often the compositions are conceived more in the manner of relief, except in the way in which the individual fields are modeled. Monumental decoration of surface, although frequently on a very small scale, was still a primary consideration except in a few informal subjects.

In general the rendering of the complete visual effect in a naturalistic manner was the aim of most of the Dutch painters of the seventeenth century, of many painters of the eighteenth century especially those, like Chardin, dealing with more homely subject matter, and it has been the generally accepted aim of painters of the nineteenth century and of the so-called "traditional" painters of the present century, whether the subjects be outdoors as in landscape, or indoors as in portrait, genre, or still life.

The painting of Vermeer represents what may be thought of as the normal use of the mode of the total visual effect, but there are many possible variations which take into account the different factors involved in the visual effect and represent existence in space beyond the plane of the picture in a naturalistic fashion. Even in this general mode painting may be far from a literal rendering of superficial effect. Some of these possible variations, especially those dealing with the different ways of treating relations of values and hues and intensities, will be more conveniently considered in a separate chapter.

---

of the mountains seen through large windows. Each photograph was made by taking first of all a long exposure of the room with the outside shutters of the facing window closed; then without moving the camera the shutters of the window were opened and a short exposure was made to take in the landscape. The result suggested more of the actual experience of being in the room and looking out at the landscape than would have been possible with the ordinary photograph. The combination of two light effects to satisfy one's idea suggested the nonliteral rendering of concept by Van Eyck.

7

VARIATIONS IN THE REPRESENTATION OF DETAIL AND IN THE TREATMENT OF TONE RELATIONS IN PAINTING

We have seen that painting, even in the mode of the total visual effect, may be far from a mere photographic imitation of the projection on the retina of the eye. Even here there may be a rendering of concept which differs from the effect of a given moment. In the actual rendering there may be still other arbitrary variations. Some of these considerations apply to more than one mode of painting and so they are taken up here in a separate chapter instead of under the different modes.

NORMAL, TELESCOPIC (OR MICROSCOPIC), AND IMPRESSIONISTIC HANDLING OF DETAIL

A painting by Vermeer, like the "Portrait of the Painter" (Plate LVIII) or the "Girl with the Pewter Jug" in the Metropolitan Museum, may be taken as an example of what may be called *normal handling* of detail. If one looks at such a painting from a distance that is convenient for seeing the whole picture, one makes out the details about as one would in looking at the subject itself. If one approaches closer to the painting, one becomes conscious of the brush strokes but obtains no more information as to detailed form.

On the other hand if one looks at a painting by Van Eyck (the "Madonna and Child with Chancellor Rolin," Plate LXIII, is a good example) from a convenient distance to see the whole picture one can not make out the detail as clearly as one does by walking up close to it and examining it bit by bit. Of course Van Eyck did not paint directly from the subject, but it is as if in looking at the subject he had used a pair of opera glasses or a telescope to make out the details more precisely than he could by naked eye, and has rendered them in this way. This may be called *telescopic handling*.

Turning to a painting like "Las Meniñas" by Velásquez, or possibly a portrait by Hals, even at a normal distance from the painting one is conscious of the brush strokes which when seen at closer range become actually difficult to interpret. In this case we have what may be called *impressionistic handling*, and we have this type of handling in much painting since Hals and Velásquez. This variation in handling has nothing to do with the essential mode of representation except that in the broader type of handling there is more emphasis on the paint surface; it is felt to be definitely a rendering in terms of paint and brush stroke. Extreme examples of broad handling are to be found in some of Cézanne's paintings in which there is an insistence on a harmony of shape and measure in the brush strokes, which he observed to be a fundamental factor in the organization of much Renaissance and Baroque painting though less obviously accented. Impressionistic handling is also to be seen in much Venetian painting like that of Titian and Tintoretto, as well as in many of the sketchily executed paintings of Pompeii and Herculaneum.

VALUE RELATIONS

It was pointed out in the last chapter that, as is well understood, the range of values in a painting seen in the diffused light of an ordinary room or picture gallery is necessarily small compared with the range of values in the subject, even in the case of an interior where the light from a window shines directly upon the objects in a room and is possibly reflected in shiny surfaces. In the case of a sunlit landscape the difference is very great indeed, although the apparent difference is not as great as the absolute difference on account of the adaptation of the eye for indoor and outdoor light. It follows that in a painting only the relations of light and dark and not the actual contrasts can be accurately rendered. On the other hand certain arbitrary distortions of the value relations have been employed in some types of painting of the past and these are not so well understood.[1] Moreover, the possible variation in intensity range in painting as compared with that in nature and the possible abstractions which may be employed in the rendering of hue relations have never been adequately discussed.

[1] Ruskin is the only writer, I believe, who has ever considered this problem at all. See *Modern Painters*, vol. IV, part V, chapter 4, "Of Turnerian Light."

Normal Rendering of Value Relations

With the narrow range of values in painting it is impossible to express the strength of contrast between the different parts of the value range in nature; and it is impossible, if the main relations are preserved, to express anything like all of the details of form which in nature are clearly brought out by the wider contrasts. On the other hand, it is possible in painting to express the main relations of light and dark with perfect accuracy, as may be seen in fig. 43, where the distances from Blk′ to D′ to M′ to Lt′ to Wt′ in painting are proportional to those in

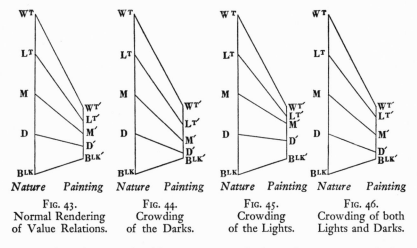

Nature Painting Nature Painting Nature Painting Nature Painting

FIG. 43.
Normal Rendering
of Value Relations.

FIG. 44.
Crowding
of the Darks.

FIG. 45.
Crowding
of the Lights.

FIG. 46.
Crowding of both
Lights and Darks.

nature, though to attain this accurate rendering of nature great judgment is required on the part of the painter, who must be something more than a mere matcher of tones. Some of the best examples of what we may call this "normal method" of rendering value relations are to be found, aside from the best works of Vermeer, in "Las Meniñas" and the "Villa Medici" by Velásquez, in some of Corot's earlier works, and in some of the paintings of Turner's middle period.

Crowding of the Darks

Let us suppose that for some reason or other the painter is not so much interested in an accurate rendering of the proportional value relations, but is especially interested in the strength of the contrasts in the lighter tones, and in the strong contrast between these and the principal darker tones. Instead of maintaining the distances of Blk to D to M to Lt to Wt in their true relation, he may extend the upper part of the value scale, and crowd the lower part, as in fig. 44. The painting will then be a distortion of the proportional relations; but it may possibly express his ideas better, or it may give him a general tonality, or make possible a type of composition which is more suitable to his particular requirements. In this case the distortion is perfectly justifiable. In all cases, of course, it is finally a question of aesthetic result. Examples of compositions based on "crowding of the darks" in this fashion are to be found in the works of Caravaggio, Ribera, Rembrandt, Hobbema, Ruysdael and other Dutch landscape painters, and of Poussin, Claude, Wilson, and Turner. In many cases, this scheme is used in connection with the rendering of an effect of concentrated light which in nature would actually produce much the same result; but it is notable that in many other paintings the same arrangement of values is maintained. Almost all seventeenth- and eighteenth-century landscape paintings show very dark masses in the foreground to set off the lighter tones of the middle distance and distance, where the main interest is concentrated; and the composition regularly proceeds from dark foreground through a series of two or three lighter planes to the distance. Even in sea pieces, like those of Van de Velde, the immediate "foreground" is regularly darkened. In landscapes the effect is often as if a huge canopy were suspended over the foreground, from under which the observer looks off into the sunlit distance. The "View of Delft" by Vermeer, in the museum at the Hague, is one of the few landscapes of the seventeenth century in which the foreground is not arbitrarily darkened and the values are rendered throughout in their normal relations.

In figure painting "crowding of the darks" usually produces a sensational effect of large masses of extreme dark, relieved by small spots of gleaming light. This effect was definitely sought for by many of the later Renaissance painters, beginning with Leonardo da Vinci. It goes along with the general sensationalism of much of this painting. In the Baroque epoch of the later sixteenth and seventeenth centuries, Caravaggio was the principal innovator in the use of concentrated light effect. Guido Reni, Guercino, and almost all of the Italian painters of the seventeenth century borrowed the scheme; it was also imitated by many of the northern painters who studied in Italy, as shown in some of the early works of Rubens and Van Dyck; and the Spanish-Neapolitan painter, Ribera, made it a principal means for the expression of his sensational conceptions.

Crowding of the Lights

Turner, in some of his later work, and other painters, like Monet for instance, though the latter often merely limited his range to higher values, have tried to achieve more of an impression of illumination in the composition as a whole by exactly reversing this process and crowding the lights, instead of the darks, as shown in fig. 45. In this case, the canvas tends on the whole to become a glare of light, with very slight contrasts and little indication of detail in the lighter portions, and with perhaps a few small accents of darker tones in the foreground. This has often been supposed to come closer to nature, but it is in reality just as arbitrary as the crowding of the darks.

Crowding of both Lights and Darks

Rembrandt, in some of his works, crowds both ends of the value range, as shown in fig. 46, sliding over the intermediate tones rapidly, and thereby increasing the effect of the contrast between light and dark. In the work of many figure and portrait painters a slight pulling-up of the darks and half-lights in the planes turned toward the light is used to increase the effect of broad illumination in such passages. Examples are to be found in the portraits of Reynolds and of other English painters. Turner was often completely arbitrary, raising the values of the shadows in certain passages and not in others to distinguish between larger areas of light opposed to masses of shadow or half tone.

I do not mean to suggest that painters have worked directly from nature, consciously distorting value relations in this way; but the various hypotheses indicated in these diagrams will serve to explain the general conceptions which, on different occasions, governed the painters' interpretations of the effect of light and dark. The drawings shown in Plate LXVII may make the distinction clearer.

INTENSITY RELATIONS

Normal Intensity Range

In a similar way it will be seen from fig. 47 that the possible intensity range in nature is much greater than that in painting, but that the relations of intensities to values in nature may be accurately expressed in their true proportion in painting. To represent the possibilities as clearly as possible, let us suppose that we have one tone in nature, *a* in fig. 48 A.

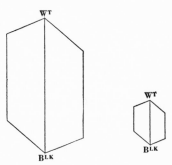

FIG. 47. Limitation of Intensity Range Corresponding to Limitation of Value Range.

Within the narrower limits of values and intensities in painting, *b* in fig. 48 B represents its intensity in relation to the value range in true proportion. This, shown also in fig. 48 B', we may call the "normal rendering of intensity relations." The "View of Delft" by Vermeer, many paintings by Corot, many by Constable, many by Turner from his middle period, a painting like the "Westminster Bridge" by Whistler, as well as many early works by Monet and Pissarro, may be cited as examples of this normal method of painting.

Suppressed Intensity Range

On the other hand, many painters, particularly landscape painters of the seventeenth and eighteenth centuries, perhaps partly on account of custom, or because of limitations of pigment materials, or for the sake of greater tone harmony, especially to accord with the general tonality of the interior decoration of the time, have arbitrarily expressed themselves in what we may call a "suppressed" intensity range. In this case *a* of fig. 48 A is represented by *c* in C. This, shown also in fig. 48 C', produces an effect of very subdued color. Relative degrees of intensity are of course represented within this narrower range. In addition to painters of the seventeenth and eighteenth centuries, who for the most part used warm golden tonalities, Whistler in the nineteenth century very frequently suppressed the range of intensities in a perfectly arbitrary fashion for the sake of greater tone harmony.

Exaggerated Intensity Range

Still other painters in recent times have attempted to express more of the positive intensity of color in nature and more of the total brilliance of outdoor contrasts by exaggerating the intensity range in

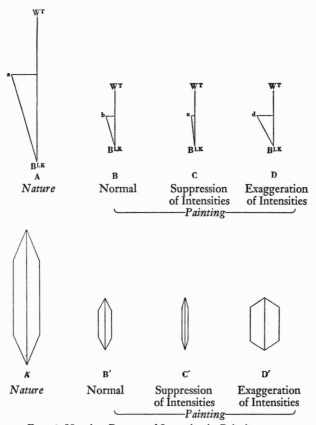

FIG. 48. Varying Ranges of Intensity in Painting.

relation to the value range. In this case *a* of fig. 48 A is rendered perhaps by *d* in D. The same idea is shown also in fig. 48 D′. By such means painters like Monet, Renoir, Dodge MacKnight, and perhaps Turner in some of his later work, though he was more often merely handling especially brilliant effects in nature in a nearly normal manner, have been able in a measure to compensate for the loss of value contrasts in painting, by substituting greater proportional hue and intensity contrasts, and in this arbitrary manner to express something of the emotional reaction which they have felt in the presence of nature. As a matter of fact most of these painters have tended to transpose the tones of nature into a harmony of highest possible brilliance, as has been suggested in an earlier chapter. They have laid out on their palettes only pigments of high intensity from red around to violet, and have mixed these only with adjacent hues or with white. This is, I believe, the real explanation of the special qualities of the palette used by Monet, instead of the pseudo-scientific theory of the breaking-up of light into all the colors of the spectrum usually offered. The transposition from nature is perfectly arbitrary. When the average untrained observer objects to the tones in these paintings as untruthful, he is usually told that this is the way the painter sees them in nature. It is nothing of the sort. The painter makes an arbitrary transposition into a scheme of his own for the sake of expressing what he considers most important in the organization of the tones in nature, and to express more convincingly his emotional reaction. Everyone has to get used to the conventions employed before he can understand what the painter is driving at. It is seldom anyone is able to understand a picture by Dodge MacKnight, for instance, the first time that he sees any of this painter's work; there are few who do not take the color in these paintings as a matter of course in a short time.

HUE RELATIONS

At the present day there is a rather generally accepted popular notion that an artist, when he paints from nature, should try to copy down the tones in his subject exactly as he sees them, rendering not only the variations of value and intensity but also all their exact variations of hue. This is what students are ordinarily taught to do, as far as is possible, in the art schools. That is what most people, I suppose, understand by the phrase "learning to paint." Moreover, the modern naturalist painter, whether "pointillistic," like Monet, or broadly impressionistic, like Sargent, has thought of his painting as an imitation of the cross section of the rays of light traveling toward the eye, in a plane at a distance corresponding to the normal distance of the picture from the eye. The so-called impressionists emphasized the main relations of the different parts of this cross section in "broken-color" technique, and ignored precise details of form and of local tone; other painters may have sought to distinguish individual objects in form and texture more completely. In any case, the object of all these painters has been to render the main variations of tone in an imitative fashion. As a matter of fact, even in the nineteenth century and at the present day, the most naturalistic painters have actually practiced within conventions much more limited than is popularly supposed, or than they themselves have imagined in many cases. Almost every painter has, in the course of time, adopted at least a more or less limited range of pigments, and has got into the habit of adapting his expression, and even his vision, to the possibilities of his particular palette. In the case of painters before the nineteenth century the idea of rendering the tones of nature in an imitative fashion probably never occurred to anyone. Painters constantly interpreted nature in a vocabulary of tone which was based on that prescribed by the master in the workshop, and was then possibly varied somewhat according to the individual painter's particular purpose. The rendering of tone was always a matter of the *expression* of what seemed essential relations within conventional limitations, and not at all a matter of an *imitation* of all the variations of hue in the subject itself.

In a drawing which shows merely the relative illumination of surface in light and shade, it is possible to express the main effect of light and shadow by an arbitrary abstraction into two values — perhaps white paper for all the lighter tones, and a wash of bistre or sepia or gray for all the tones that are on the whole dark, although there may be a considerable range of values in both lights and darks in the subject itself. Some of Tiepolo's wash drawings illustrate this method of abstract expression. We should be making use of much the same sort of abstraction if, in a painting, we were to express all the different warm tones in a subject by some one warm hue, perhaps orange, and all the cool tones by some one cool hue, perhaps blue or green-blue, as shown in the diagram in fig. 49 A. We may draw a dividing line anywhere we like — letting O stand for all hues on one side of the line, and B for all the hues on the other side. In this case the line suggested is through YG–N–VR. If we use orange and blue pigments, with white and black, to obtain different values, we may mix the orange and the blue together to get different intensities of each hue, or possibly neutral — any tone, that is, along the line O–N–B. By varying intensities of the orange and blue along this line, we may actually indicate a good deal of the essential effect of color in a composition; by inference — that is, by association in this case — we may even suggest some actual variation of hue beyond the two employed. Essentially, however, it is

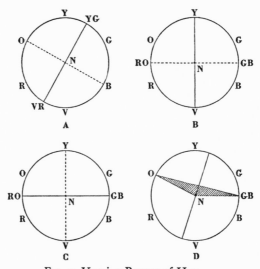

Fig. 49. Varying Ranges of Hue.

an abstract rendering of merely the main relations of warm and cool tones, without regard to exact variations of hue. For many purposes this may be all that we want — in fact, on account of the ease of expression or the harmony of tone involved, it may be preferable in many cases to an attempt to render all the variations of hue that exist in the subject itself.

One may make an arbitrary rendering of hue in this way with any pair of complementary hues, according to the particular tonality in the subject which it may be desirable to emphasize, as in fig. 49 B and C; or one may use approximate complementaries as is indicated in fig. 49 D. In this case the mixture of the two hues will give low intensities of the intermediate hues on one side of neutral; but the abstraction is nearly as complete as with exact complementaries.

Common examples of such abstract renderings of main hue relations, as, for example, red and neutral, are to be found in the reproductions on certain magazine covers. Some of the colored motion pictures have also been based on an abstraction into a warm hue like red-orange and a cool hue like green-blue. These might or might not be exact complementaries in subtractive mixing; they would probably give a slightly more naturalistic effect, if they were not exact complementaries.

In the painting of the Renaissance this kind of abstract rendering of hue is often found. Good examples are the landscape backgrounds in some of the Florentine and Umbro-Florentine paintings of the fifteenth century, as in those by Antonio Pollaiuolo and Piero della Francesca. In these it is a mere matter of play of hue and intensity obtained by the use of brownish and bluish pigments — usually a low intensity orange or orange-yellow, and a green-blue. In the distances of some of the landscapes by Claude Lorrain and Poussin in the seventeenth century it also seems to come down frequently to an abstraction into a relative warm and a relative cool obtained by brown and blue pigments.

It is frequently pointed out by psychologists that a small field of neutral gray placed in the middle of a field of color will, by inference, appear to be the complementary hue in a low intensity. So if we place a neutral in the midst of a field of red, or red-orange, the neutral will tell as a positively cool tone, GB or B. Therefore the hues in a subject might be rendered abstractly by a mere play of a warm tone and the relatively cool tone of neutral.

From the sixteenth century down through the later Renaissance the variations of warm and cool hues in flesh tone and even in a whole subject are constantly rendered in precisely this way, in a play of neutral (white and black) with a red or a red-orange, or, as in some Baroque paintings, even orange or orange-yellow, sometimes perhaps with some accents of yellow. The "Athenaeum Portrait of Washington," by Gilbert Stuart, in the Museum of Fine Arts in Boston, is a good illustration of the possibilities of such abstraction. The eyes, for example, tell as decided blue; but this is achieved only with a mixture of white and black paint, relieved against the ruddy flesh tone.

If one were to add a yellow pigment to the palette of red and neutral just suggested, one would still have a decidedly limited and abstract palette, as shown in fig. 50; but it would lend itself to a suggestion of considerably more variety of hue. In this case there would be a distinct harmonization of hues within the approximate smaller circle. The mixtures of pigments — perhaps Venetian red, yellow ochre, and white and black — would achieve actual tones within the triangle R′–Y′–B′, which is a decided positive harmony of hue and intensity in the painting surface as a whole, if one has regard for its significance as decoration in a room; but, as in this general tonality the positive neutral would tell as a low intensity blue, relative neutral in the painting would be repre-

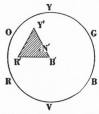

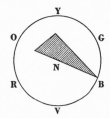

FIG. 50. Limited Range of Hue and Intensity in Much Renaissance Painting.

FIG. 51. Limited Range of Hue and Intensity used in Certain Types of Landscape Painting.

sented by a positive orange or orange-yellow. Therefore within the positive harmony of hue and intensity we might have an expression or indication of a considerable variety of color — thus orange between R′ and Y′, green between Y′ and B′, and even a definite suggestion of violet between R′ and B′, B′ in this case being actually a neutral obtained by a mixture of white and black pigments. In the Ross Collection at the Boston Museum there are two small paintings of landscapes with figures, probably by some Italian painter of about 1700,[2] in which there is an effect of great variety as well as richness of color. In these paintings there are tones which tell as decided blues and greens and violets, along with the warmer tones of reds and browns and yellows, and one would offhand suppose that a blue pigment must have been used in painting them; but, by actual experiment, it has been found that the tones which tell as decided blues can be obtained by a mixture of white and black, and that mixtures of this neutral with yellow and

[2] These are now attributed to Pierfrancesco Mola.

red produce the relative greens and violets. Limited palettes similar to this, which conditioned an abstract rendering of hue relations, were used constantly during the later Renaissance, from the sixteenth to the end of the eighteenth century, and even in many paintings of the nineteenth century, especially those which derived from an adaptation of earlier Renaissance tonalities. Such palettes meant a very decided harmony of hue and intensity in the painting as a whole, and the resulting tonality usually fitted in very well with the general decorative schemes of the rooms in the houses and palaces of the later Renaissance. More extended ranges were also used, with positive greens and blues; usually, however, these were not very intense, and violets and blue-violets were ordinarily left out entirely, so that the range of hues and intensities was always fairly limited. Pictorial color was based for the most part on a harmony of orange or orange-yellow tonality.

Practically none of the painting of the Renaissance, even at its most naturalistic, was a matching of hues in the manner assumed popularly at the present day. It was always a transposition into a more or less restricted vocabulary, often highly abstract. Naturally, the tonal vocabulary is found to be much more conventional if one goes back to the completely non-naturalistic painting done before the sixteenth century.

What has been said above suggests something of the kind of abstract rendering of color common to painting in the later Renaissance. Many variations are of course possible. In much landscape painting of the seventeenth, eighteenth, and early nineteenth centuries, as in the early Turners and in many Corots, one finds a limited hue and intensity range something like that indicated in fig. 51, which would depend on the use of a brown pigment, like burnt sienna, a yellow like yellow ochre, and a blue like Prussian or cobalt blue. A Venetian red, instead of burnt sienna, might be used to extend the palette down to red-orange; or Venetian red and Indian red, or even vermilion, might be used for occasional small accents, as in the figures, without altering the general scheme.

A combination of red, yellow, and blue pigments is frequently used in painting. Even with high intensities, this means more limitation of hue and intensity than is often supposed, for the orange, green, and violet intermediates cannot be achieved in quite the intensities of the main red, yellow, and blue tones. With low intensities of the main tones, the limitations are naturally greater throughout.

Other "triads" of hue might also be used, as indicated in fig. 52, which shows the most obvious ones to be derived from the scale of twelve hues. Each of these presents a special case of limitation of intensity, according to what are taken as main hues and what as intermediates. Sets of three hues taken at unequal, instead of equal, intervals in the

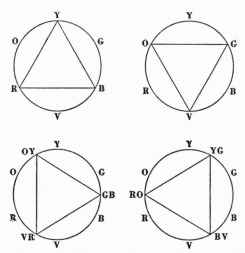

FIG. 52. Limitation of Hue and Intensity in Principal Triads.

twelve-hue scale might also be used, as in fig. 51, which has already been referred to. Also the intensities may be varied. Using only three hues in this way, the variations possible are almost endless; but the use of any one involves a more or less arbitrary transposition from the tones of nature into those of the painting.

As a matter of fact, a naturalistic effect may be maintained even when the abstraction is carried still farther in some ways than it was in the painting of the Renaissance. For instance, it was stated at the beginning of this chapter that one might abstract all the warm and cool tones in a subject into two hues, one warm and one cool, and still obtain in many cases a good deal of natural effect. Suppose that in making a painting in this way we were to use a red-orange for the warm tones and a green-blue for the cool tones. If we were to paint in oils, we could make our painting very conveniently by arranging our palette, very much after the manner of later Renaissance painters, in a series of different values of red-orange on one side, and different values of green-blue on the other, as in fig. 53.

WT				WT			WT	
RO	(HLT)	GB		Y	V		V	Y
RO	(LT)	GB		OY	BV		VR	YG
RO	(LLT)	GB		O	B		R	G
RO	(M)	GB		RO	GB		RO	GB
RO	(HD)	GB		R	G		O	B
RO	(D)	GB		VR	YG		OY	BV
RO	(LD)	GB		V	Y		Y	V
	BLK				BLK		BLK	

FIG. 53. Palette of Complementary Pairs.

FIG. 54. Palettes with Different Complementary Pairs in Successive Values.

With this arrangement we can easily get any value and any intensity of the warm or cool hue that we require by mixing the tones straight across, controlling the intensity of the RO by its complementary GB, or the other way round, neutralizing the GB as required by mixing in RO at the same value, or by mixing adjacent tones up and down for intermediate values. In fig. 53 we have indicated a palette of seven registers, or value levels, between white and black. With an arrangement of this sort we shall be able to suggest a good deal of complete color effect; but we may find the result too monotonous for some purposes, in that exactly the same hue combinations are repeated at all the different values between white and black.

To avoid this monotony, suppose that instead of using red-orange and green-blue all the way up and down, we change the hues slightly from register to register, but still keep a complementary pair of hues, and so an abstraction into two hues, to represent opposite sides of the hue circle in each value level or register. We should then have a palette like one of those in fig. 54.

In each of these examples we have the possibility of expressing relative hue and intensity by the mixing of complementary pairs at the different value levels; but there is a gradual sequence of hue up and down the value registers — a perfectly ordered arrangement, but one that gives greater variety than the repetitions of the same hues in fig. 53.

This is carrying the idea of abstract expression of hue and intensity relations a bit farther than it was carried in the Renaissance; but the general idea involved is precisely the same. A completely naturalistic effect may be obtained within the limits of such abstract palettes, which offer the advantages of a simplified vocabulary of tone and at the same time ensure some definite ordering of the tones from the standpoint of design.

What has been written above suggests something of the fundamental principles involved in the use of limited vocabularies of tone in all types of painting. In practically all painting there is more or less abstraction in the expression of hue relations. The arrangements of tones on the palette shown in figs. 53 and 54 may be thought of as scaled palettes, or tone sequences. The use of these may more conveniently be discussed in a separate chapter.

8

THE USE OF LIMITED PALETTES OR LIMITED TONE SEQUENCES

INTRODUCTORY

As suggested in the last chapter, there is nothing particularly new in the use of limited ranges of tone in painting, or in the laying-out of the palette in a precise and orderly fashion to facilitate the actual work of preparing the proper tones and putting them on the canvas, panel, or wall. This was a common procedure throughout the Renaissance and down to the end of the eighteenth century. During all this time the artist was trained in the actual practice of painting in the workshop of the master; and from his master he acquired a vocabulary of tone by which to express himself, just as Renaissance artists acquired a vocabulary of line largely by copying the drawings of the master.

In the nineteenth century, for a variety of causes, the artist came to be trained in a different way. The art school largely took the place of the workshop, and the idea of complete imitation of the visual image took the place of the expression of essential relations within abstract limits, subordinated more or less to exigencies of design.[1]

---

[1] The essential difference between the imitative point of view and the point of view underlying the use of a limited vocabulary of tone to express essential relationships may perhaps be made more clear by the following explanation.

Suppose that in a given subject the main tones of light, half-light, and shadow are a, b and c, to be represented in the painting by a', b', and c' respectively, and that the orderly relationship of these tones to each other in the subject is its significant feature, the most important thing to stress in the painting. Working in the imitative manner, the painter would proceed to match these tones one by one separately, the attention being focused on getting a' in the painting like a in the subject and b' like b and so on. If this were accurately done, the relation of a' to b' to c' in the painting would be the same as the relation of a to b to c in the subject. However, as often happens in this kind of painting, where the attention is directed on the likeness of individual tones and not so much on their relation, one or more of the tones in the painting will be a bit off, or more likely a great deal off, so that the ordered relationship of the tones in the subject is lost. Re-

Something of the older idea, however, seems to have survived to some extent in certain of the studios of the nineteenth century. Certainly the so-called "Impressionist" painters in their earlier work in the sixties and seventies still emphasized the abstract rendering of form in terms of paint and brush stroke and they used fairly limited ranges of hue and intensity based often, as in the case of Manet, on the study of sixteenth- and seventeenth-century painting. Some painters attempted to recover something of what might be called the "expressional" methods and ideas of the Renaissance. Whistler probably went farther than almost any other painter in experimenting with definite arrangements of tone which he laid out on his palette and used in an abstract rendering of hue and intensity relations. But Whistler had no follower who understood what he was driving at, and so he remains one of the isolated experimenters of the nineteenth century. Painters like Pissarro, Monet, and Renoir had in mind a more complete naturalism, rather than arbitrary limitation in the manner of Whistler; nevertheless their palettes were decidedly abstract, for the tones they employed in their

---

touching is then in order to try to "pull the tones together" with the result that the paint surface is apt to be uneven in quality or entirely disordered.

The other point of view is to fasten attention on the organized relationship of the tones in the subject and to express this within the limits of a definite tonal vocabulary but without regard to whether a' is exactly like a, or b' and c' exactly like b and c, so long as this relationship is kept.

It might be put in this way:

In A the attention is focused on the correspondence indicated by the horizontal lines. In B the attention is focused on the relationship indicated by the vertical lines. One may get pretty close to achieving A and still miss the essential organization. One can achieve the essential organization indicated in B without at all obtaining in the painting any exact imitation of the separate tones of the subject. In fact one may transpose the whole subject into a tonality based on a limited arrangement of the palette in such a way that while the essential organization of the subject is rendered, the individual tones are very far removed from the corresponding ones in the subject. This was done constantly in painting down to the beginning of the nineteenth century and also in some of that of the nineteenth century; but the imitative point of view was adopted in the usual teaching in the art schools.

typical work of the eighties were limited approximately to the upper surface of the tone solid — that is, tones at full intensity, or between full intensity and white, with juxtaposition of these at about the same value level.

In the painting of the Renaissance and even in that of the later nineteenth century, as in the case of Whistler and of Monet and Renoir, the use of limited ranges of tone was largely empirical; it was merely a matter of workshop tradition or of individual experiment with pigment materials, with little theoretical basis. About fifty years ago Dr. Denman W. Ross began a series of experiments in the use of definitely arranged palettes founded on a study of Renaissance and Baroque painting but based also on a theoretical classification of tone relations without which such experiments would have been impossible. These experiments were published in a succession of books, which, considered historically, take their place as part of the general modern reaction against the over-imitative aims of much nineteenth-century painting.[2] Further study of the possibilities of representation in such palettes has been continued by some of Dr. Ross's successors in the Department of Fine Arts at Harvard. It is not my present purpose to go into an elaborate discussion of the various experiments that have been made by Dr. Ross and others in connection with the use of different palettes; but I wish to propose a simple classification of all possible palettes into a few main types, which will, I think, make the fundamental principles involved in the use of all scaled palettes — both those based on a theoretical classification of tones and those based on workshop tradition — more easily understood.

All definitely arranged palettes that can be used in representational painting owe their virtue to a regular repetition of certain hue relations at different value levels between white and black.[3] The different tones of the palette are mixed up separately and placed on the palette in a regular order, making a definite set of tones within the limits of which the painting may be produced. The range of hues and of inten-

[2] *A Theory of Pure Design* (*op. cit.*), *On Drawing and Painting* (Boston and New York, 1912) and *The Painter's Palette* (Boston and New York, 1919).

[3] Such palettes assume the use of oil paint, or of tempera or fresco, or the like. In transparent water color limited ranges of hue and intensity may be used, but the value depends on the thinness or thickness obtained by the actual manipulation of washes or touches.

sities, as well as the width of the steps from value to value and from hue to hue, may be varied practically to infinity, but on the whole the scales fall into two main types, which we may call Type A and Type B respectively.

TYPE A

What may for convenience be called Type A scales include those in which there is a repetition of the same hues in a regular succession of values, known as value registers. The same hues occur in the same relation in each value register.

Three or More Hues

In what we may call triad scales, there are three hues in each value register. Ordinarily it will be found most convenient to choose these hues at approximately equal intervals in the hue circle; but any set of three may be used, as illustrated in fig. 55. The hues and the approxi-

	WT		
HLT	R	Y	B
LT	R	Y	B
LLT	R	Y	B
M	R	Y	B
HD	R	Y	B
D	R	Y	B
LD	R	Y	B
	BLK		

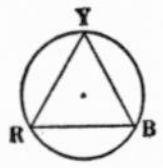

	WT		
	O	G	V
	O	G	V
	O	G	V
	O	G	V
	O	G	V
	O	G	V
	O	G	V
	BLK		

	WT		
	VR	OY	GB
	VR	OY	GB
	VR	OY	GB
	VR	OY	GB
	VR	OY	GB
	VR	OY	GB
	VR	OY	GB
	BLK		

A   B   C

	WT		
RO	YG	BV
RO	YG	BV
RO	YG	BV
RO	YG	BV
RO	YG	BV
RO	YG	BV
RO	YG	BV
	BLK	

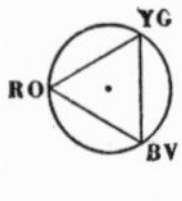

	WT		
	O	Y	B
	O	Y	B
	O	Y	B
	O	Y	B
	O	Y	B
	O	Y	B
	O	Y	B
	BLK		

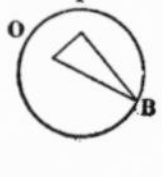

	WT		
	R	Y	N
	R	Y	N
	R	Y	N
	R	Y	N
	R	Y	N
	R	Y	N
	R	Y	N
	BLK		

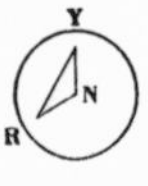

D   E   F

FIG. 55. Type A Palettes — Triads.

mate intensities, which can be obtained by mixing in each register, are shown in the circular diagrams below the different scales. Intensities may be controlled and neutrals obtained by mixing across the center, or a separate column of neutrals might be used. The intensity of the original tones of the scale may be varied indefinitely, according to the pigments employed. In fig. 55E is represented the scale which would be made by limiting the pigments employed to burnt sienna, yellow ochre, cobalt blue, white, and possibly black. This is about the range of hue and intensity to be found in much landscape painting of the seventeenth, eighteenth, and early nineteenth centuries.

Four or even five or more hues may be used. Many of the palettes of the seventeenth and eighteenth centuries would probably show several columns of hues something like that shown in fig. 56 or variations of this if they were plotted out in diagrammatic form. Probably fewer registers were used and not so systematically arranged.

		Wᴛ		
R	Y	G	B	N
R	Y	G	B	N
R	Y	G	B	N
R	Y	G	B	N
R	Y	G	B	N
R	Y	G	B	N
R	Y	G	B	N
		Bʟᴋ		

Fig. 56.

Complementary Pairs

Instead of three or more hues in each register, two hues which are complementary, or nearly so, may be used (fig. 57). This makes possible only a very limited range of hue and intensity; but, as was pointed out in the last chapter, it is surprising how much naturalism of effect can be produced by the expression merely of different intensities in tones relatively warm and relatively cool. It is an abstract method of representation, in which all the possible hues are generalized into two opposing hues on either side of the hue circle. G and H in fig. 57 illustrate approximately hue ranges to be found in some of the landscape backgrounds of early Renaissance paintings, and in some landscape paintings of the seventeenth century. In fig. 57I, the range of hue is similar to that found in much of the painting of flesh in fresco and tempera in the Renaissance; the same scheme was probably used in the underpainting for flesh in some types of painting in the later Renaissance. Fig. 57J represents a scale limited in hue to R and N, as approximately in the flesh tones in much Venetian and Baroque painting. The addition of Y would turn the whole painting into a triad scheme based on R, Y, and N, similar to the arrangement shown in fig. 55F.

Wᴛ	Wᴛ	Wᴛ	Wᴛ	Wᴛ
Y V	OY BV	O B	RO GB	R G
Y V	OY BV	O B	RO GB	R G
Y V	OY BV	O B	RO GB	R G
Y V	OY BV	O B	RO GB	R G
Y V	OY BV	O B	RO GB	R G
Y V	OY BV	O B	RO GB	R G
Y V	OY BV	O B	RO GB	R G
Bʟᴋ	Bʟᴋ	Bʟᴋ	Bʟᴋ	Bʟᴋ
A	B	C	D	E

Wᴛ	Wᴛ	Wᴛ	Wᴛ	Wᴛ
VR YG	O GB	OY B	RO G	R N
VR YG	O GB	OY B	RO G	R N
VR YG	O GB	OY B	RO G	R N
VR YG	O GB	OY B	RO G	R N
VR YG	O GB	OY B	RO G	R N
VR YG	O GB	OY B	RO G	R N
VR YG	O GB	OY B	RO G	R N
Bʟᴋ	Bʟᴋ	Bʟᴋ	Bʟᴋ	Bʟᴋ
F	G	H	I	J

Fɪɢ. 57. Type A Palettes — Complementary Pairs.

In all the scales indicated above, as well as in those of Type B which follow, variations in the intensity of a given hue depend on a mixing with the complementary hue or with neutral in the same or the adjacent registers. For certain types of painting, a scale might be made in which the relative intensities of the main planes of light, half-light, and shadow, for the modeling of each object, would be fixed on the palette. In this case, there would be a separate column of tones for each field in the painting. For a yellow drapery, for example, as shown in fig. 58, the adjustment of values and intensities would follow the general scheme of the diagram in fig. 33. Any desired number of tones from the line Y–Blk could be set out on the palette — three or four would ordinarily be sufficient — for the modeling from the plane of light down to the deep shadows. High lights would come from the line Y–Wt. The tone of each object in the plane of light is in this manner placed on the palette, and then the darker and lighter tones required determined from this. A scheme somewhat like this was possibly used by Vermeer. In his painting the fields are quite distinct, and reflections are ignored to some extent; but the intensities in the different planes of

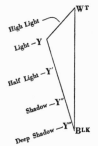

				WT	
				Y	V
				OY	BV
				O	B
				RO	GB
				R	G
				VR	YG
				V	Y
				BLK	

FIG. 58. Diagram for Tones of Single Hue in a Palette Designed to Show Proportional Diminution of Intensities in Each Field.

FIG. 59. Type B Palette — Complementary Pairs with Warm Hues at Full Intensity.

light are very carefully adjusted to render clearly the proportional diminution of values and intensities as objects model down into shadow. In this case the different tones from light to dark are of uniform purity or approximately so. In such painting the reflection of one object in the surface of another, or the reflection of light from the surface of one object on that of another may be rendered by a slight playing together of the scales of the separate objects.[4] In painting of this sort, there will be little of the harmony of tone referred to later on, which is due to the feeling of a single palette forming the basis for all the tones in the composition; moreover, there is a danger of getting an overmonotonous effect in the separate fields in place of the play or vibration of hues that can be obtained by the use of the more usual palettes; but feeling of

[4] In *Modern Color*, by C. G. Cutler and S. C. Pepper (Cambridge, Mass., 1923), the use of a color top to ensure an accurate carrying down of the tones toward black and up to white is suggested since pigments mixed with white tend often to go up to white on a curved instead of a straight line. The frequent neutralization in the half-light as an object rounds into shadow, may also be worked out in this way.

existence in space and atmosphere may be achieved with this palette. Harmony will depend on the exactness of the adjustment of value and intensity relations, and on the adjustment of the attractions formed by the contrasts between the tones of the different fields.

TYPE B

What may be distinguished as Type B scales include those in which there is a regular sequence of hue from register to register, with the relations of hue within the separate registers remaining approximately uniform, as illustrated in fig. 59 and in others following.

Complementary Pairs

In fig. 57D is shown a scale in which RO and GB are repeated in all the different registers. In fig. 59, RO and GB are kept in the M register, but in the register next above the complementary pair is changed to that of O and B, the next above that to OY and BV, and the next to Y and V. With the same movement continued downward below middle, the scale shown in fig. 59 is formed. This is the same as

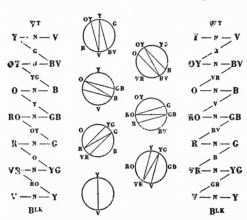

in fig. 54 in the preceding chapter. In this the expression in each register is limited to the range of a complementary pair, as in Type A scales; but in the scale as a whole there is a much greater variety of hue, though limited to a very definite sequence. Furthermore, still greater variety of hue may be obtained by

FIG. 60. Type B Palette with Indication of Tones Derived by Mixing Adjacents.

mixing between registers on diagonals, as seen in fig. 60; but the tones here fall also into very definite sequences of hue. In this scale, the hues Y, OY, O, RO, R, VR, V, all come at their normal value levels in the tone solid, and may be obtained at their highest intensities.

Another scale may be made in which we also keep RO and GB in the M register, but in which we proceed in the registers above to G and R, then YG and VR, and Y and V, in order, and below, to B and O, BV and OY, and V and Y, as in fig. 61. In this scale, Y, YG, G, GB, B, BV, and V come at their normal value levels, and each one of these may be obtained at its highest intensity. The tones obtained by mixture in this scale are shown in fig. 62. In this, as in the preceding scale, a great variety of hues may be obtained, but also all within definite sequences.

Either one of these scales may be used separately, or they may be used together, as long as they are not mixed across so as to destroy the feeling of the sequences which are clearly indicated in all the vertical series in figs. 60 and 62. The arrangement of the palette in this case is shown in fig. 63.

Wᴛ

V	Y
VR	YG
R	G
RO	GB
O	B
OY	BV
Y	V

Bʟᴋ

Fɪɢ. 61. Type B Palette — Complementary Pairs with Cool Hues at Full Intensity.

This palette, with the possible variations in its use, is discussed at length in Dr. Ross's *The Painter's Palette*. The two scales, either together or singly, have been used for several years in the courses in painting in Harvard University; they are, I believe, especially satisfactory for the beginner, for, although they are very abstract and necessitate definite thinking and clean handling, taken together they command a wide range of hue and intensity. For many purposes, other perhaps more limited palettes have the advantage of greater simplicity. Successful use of such sequences depends on careful laying out of the palette so that the tones in each register are the same value and the steps between registers are even.

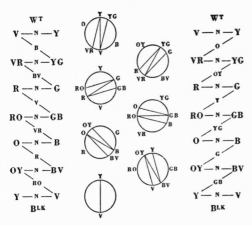

Fɪɢ. 62. Type B Palette with Indication of Tones Derived by Mixing Adjacents.

MODES OF REPRESENTATION

By varying the value levels of the complementary pairs, other similar scales may be formed. If Y and V, for example, are placed in the M register, the two scales shown in fig. 64 will be formed. Keeping to seven value registers between Wt and Blk, as in the simple value

Wt		Wt			Wt		Wt	
Y	V	V	Y		RO	GB	GB	RO
OY	BV	VR	YG		O	B	G	R
O	B	R	G		OY	BV	YG	VR
RO	GB	RO	GB		Y	V	Y	V
R	G	O	B		YG	VR	OY	BV
VR	YG	OY	BV		G	R	O	B
V	Y	Y	V		GB	RO	RO	GB
Blk		Blk			Blk		Blk	

FIG. 63. Double Type B Palettes with RO and GB at M.   FIG. 64. Double Type B Palettes with Y and V at M.

scale described in Chapter 1, twelve different scales may be formed on this principle. With variations in the number of value registers and in the intervals between the hues, different scales of this type, all perfectly orderly and perfectly usable, may be formed practically to infinity.

Triads

Triad arrangements of hues may be used in Type B scales also. A few examples are given in fig. 65. These also may be varied endlessly.

	Wt				Wt		
R	Y	B		R	Y	B
VR	OY	GB		RO	YG	BV
V	O	G		O	G	V
BV	RO	YG		OY	GB	VR
B	R	Y		Y	B	R
GB	VR	OY		YG	BV	RO
G	V	O		G	V	O
	Blk				Blk		

FIG. 65. Type B Palettes — Triads.

In general, however, scales of this sort are almost too cumbersome; they offer more tones than are really needed. As triad or similar arrangements are usually the best for ordinary purposes in Type A scales, so the complementary pair arrangements are usually the more satisfactory in Type B scales.

VARIATIONS IN ARRANGEMENT AND USE OF SCALED PALETTES

No matter how scales may be worked out, so long as they have definite order in them, they will be found to fall into one of these main classes, called here Type A and Type B respectively. The exact intervals between values and between hues may, as pointed out above, be varied indefinitely.

In all the scales described in the preceding pages, the tones within each value register are all placed at the same value; but a sequence of

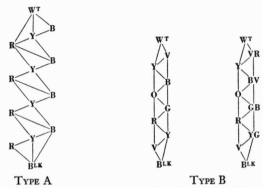

TYPE A   TYPE B

FIG. 66. Palettes with a Sequence of Values in each Register.
NOTE: Mixtures on the palette would naturally be confined to those indicated by the connecting lines.

values might be established in each register, as in fig. 66. An arrangement of this sort is especially advantageous, if the scale is composed of only a few registers.

The definite use of scales in actual painting cannot ordinarily be learned without some personal instruction; but in general it may be stated that the tones, having once been fixed on the palette, may be mixed on the palette, or they may be mixed entirely on the canvas, or they may be juxtaposed on the canvas practically without mixing, as in well-established practices of handling. It is better, however, to mix as little as possible on the palette, for intimate mixing is likely to lower the value below that of the tones mixed, especially if high intensities are employed. An experienced painter will ordinarily mix his tones to a large extent on his brush, picking up the right amount of adjacent tones so that the stroke, without producing an intimate mixture, will give the tone required. This of course results in a combining of partly subtractive and partly additive mixture. Refinements may be achieved by overlaying or interknitting of strokes in the wet paint without destroying the freshness of quality. One matter to which few painters at the present day pay sufficient attention is the necessity for uniform handling over the whole surface of a painting. This is a most important consideration, for, unless the details in all parts of the composition are handled with the same degree of minuteness, there will be a distinct feeling of inharmonious scale of handling in the composition as a whole. The handling may be broad, or it may be fine; it must be uniform or it must be varied according to some definite system of focus. It should not be minute in one place and broad in another without definite reason; it should not be hard-edged in one part and soft-edged in others. Almost all of the French and Italian paintings of the eighteenth century are notable for their harmonious scale of handling. Even the skies or flat wall surfaces are painted in such a way that there is in them a feeling of the same measure of touch as in the modeling of a face or in the indication of the texture of a lace collar.

One great advantage in the use of scaled palettes is that a painter may think out the whole tone arrangement of his work before starting to paint, and may then execute the various fields independently, working steadily from day to day, without the necessity of final retouching. Moreover, a painter may think out his work in such a way that he may easily paint from imagination or on the basis of drawings made from nature. A portrait may be painted on the basis of a drawing made at perhaps only one sitting, without the necessity for further sittings, in the manner followed by Holbein and other painters of the Renaissance. Notes in regard to the various local tones, like those made by Holbein, as an aid to the memory, are all that is required. On the basis of such a definite procedure, fresh and uniform quality of surface may be achieved over a whole composition. This was very much the regular procedure followed by all painters down to the close of the eighteenth century, and this accounts for the difference in quality between the work of even a minor painter before the end of the eighteenth century and the typical work even of the greatest men of the nineteenth century. Muddying of quality results necessarily from the usual practice in vogue at the present day of approximating the main masses of a

composition over the whole surface, and then correcting and rework-
ing in endless repainting over the top. No painting can be satisfactory
in quality unless every stroke from the canvas up is in its right place,
calculated to play its proper part in the final effect. The modern painter
can ordinarily achieve fresh quality only in a quick sketch.[5]

USE OF SCALED PALETTES IN THE RENAISSANCE

That the masters of the Renaissance used palettes which were carefully arranged in something of the manner of the more precisely scaled
palettes discussed above, may be observed by a careful examination of
their works; but on account of the overlaying and mixing of tones in
the final painting, it is usually impossible to tell exactly what all the
original tones on the palette may have been, or exactly how they were
used, though at times it is probably possible to come surprisingly close
to it. Usually, when artists or other persons came to write about painting, they found it too difficult to describe their technical procedures in
words — partly, no doubt, because they had no definite terms for the
different factors that enter into tone — and, although frequently dis-
cussing pigment materials and their preparation in detail, they were
apt to pass over the far more important part of the subject, which refers
to the laying-out of the palette and the way in which the tones were
mixed and applied in actual painting, with the remark that this could
be learned only by practice under a master. Occasionally, however,
writers have attempted to give more detailed information in regard to
the way in which pigments were laid out on the palette, or arranged
in jars, as in painting in fresco and tempera, and how these were used
in practice. As at the present day we unfortunately have no masters,
at least in the sense in which those of the Renaissance were masters,
these accounts are of the greatest interest in supplementing the information which we may obtain from the paintings themselves.

Of all these accounts that of Cennino Cennini [6] is the fullest and
in many ways the most important. The procedures which he describes
are those of fourteenth- and fifteenth-century painters in fresco and
tempera, and although these cannot be applied directly to painting at

---

[5] Examples of the use of most of the different palettes discussed may be seen
by anyone interested at the Fogg Art Museum of Harvard University.
[6] *Op. cit.*

the present day, unless it is archaistic in style, he gives us a valuable insight into the systematic character of Medieval and Renaissance performance which had so much to do with the final quality of the painting, and some of his directions apply to all painting. There are also fragmentary accounts of later Renaissance procedures in certain books written in the seventeenth and eighteenth centuries. So far, however, investigators in going through these documents have confined their attention almost exclusively to the question of pigment materials and media, or else to general aesthetic questions about which the seventeenth- and eighteenth-century artists did such a lot of inconclusive talking and writing. A careful search of documents of the later Renaissance from the point of view of scaled palettes might be most instructive.[7] One or two passages such as I have in mind will be referred to presently.

In the painting of the Middle Ages and the earlier Renaissance a distinct scale was usually employed for each of the separate fields of the composition. Cennino describes very clearly how this was done in the fourteenth century. A red drapery, for example, was painted by preparing three main tones for the three main planes of light, half-light, and shadow: red with a very small touch of white for the shadow, more white for the half-light, and still more white for the light. The value and intensity relations of this scale are shown in fig. 41. White, or white with a little red, would be used for a few touches of high light, and red alone, or with a little black, for a few accents of deep shadow. The highest intensity of hue came in the shadow. Draperies of blue or of other hues were painted in a similar manner. Flesh was painted in a combination of different values of red, or red-orange, and green or yellow-green. This procedure described by Cennino continued in use in much of the Italian painting of the fifteenth and even of the sixteenth century. Sometimes, however, it was varied. Yellow, instead of white, was sometimes used to produce the lighter tones in painting a drapery, producing in the case of the reddish drapery a sequence of hue from R in shadow, to O or RO in half-light, to Y or OY in the light. In another drapery, the sequence of hue might be from B in shadow, to GB or G in half-light, to YG or Y in the light. Sequences

[7] Since the above was written a new book has appeared which supplies considerable information on this subject: *The Practice of Painting*, by F. Schmid (London, 1948). See Bibliographical Note.

of hue of this sort are to be found also in Byzantine mosaics, and in tapestries and embroideries of the Renaissance. They might be classed as Type B scales.

The painters of the sixteenth and seventeenth centuries continued to handle their separate fields almost independently, but there seems to be little written record of the procedures of this time. In Venetian painting of the sixteenth century, a system of opaque underpainting, with occasional superposed transparent glazes, was used. For the flesh, the painting was apparently often executed entirely in white, black, and red, or red-orange, a limited range of tone similar to that shown in scale J in fig. 57. Other tones were obtained by means of glazes over the underpainting, or by variations in the tone of the underpainting.[8] Simple opaque underpaintings with occasional superposed glazes in the manner of Venetian painting were used extensively in the later Renaissance. The work of Lely illustrates this method especially clearly. Sometimes, especially for cool tones, the underpainting was apparently simply neutral, in mixtures of white and black pigments, with glazes of blue or green above. Gradually, however, painters came to lay out their whole palettes in an arrangement of tones which, with slight variations and a certain amount of glazing, could be used as a basis for the painting of all the different fields of a composition. This may be seen in the work of Rubens, and more especially in that of painters of the eighteenth century, like Tiepolo or Boucher, who constantly used palettes in red, yellow, and blue, similar to that shown in scale A in fig. 55, but with an extra column of neutrals with which the different colored tones would ordinarily be mixed (as in fig. 56). Some writers of the eighteenth century speak of the necessity of having a picture appear as if it were all painted with a single palette.[9]

[8] In the work of Titian, Tintoretto, and Veronese, toward the end of the sixteenth century, there was often a building-up of the final effect in an alternation of scumbling (opaque light over dark) and glazing, that was as far removed as possible from any imitative procedure.

[9] "Les couleurs doivent avoir quelque correspondance entre'elles, une perpetuelle union, les unes avec les autres, ce qu'on appelle aussi l'entente des couleurs; c'est pourquoi l'on dit qu'il faudrait qu'un Tableau fut peint d'une seule Palette." (*Traité sur la peinture*, par Me. Bernard du Puy du Grez, 1700.)

"M. Jouvenet portait souvent la couleur de ses chairs pour rompre ses draperies et pour les accorder ensemble; cela revient à l'unisson et produit en partie les effets dont je viens de parler. Il est certain que si toutes ces couleurs participent les unes

A description of what is probably a typical seventeenth-century palette I have found in a book called *Les premiers éléments de la peinture pratique*, by J. B. Corneille, Peintre de l'Académie Royale, published in 1684. This palette is one arranged especially for painting a head, but Corneille explains that other fields are to be painted in a similar manner. A simple set of pigments is arranged along the outer edge of the palette, beginning with the lighter ones near the thumbhole and ending with the darker ones farther away at the left end of the palette. On the main part of the palette are then mixed up two sets of tones, one called "jours," the other "demi-teintes" and "ombres," to correspond roughly to the warmer tones of the lights and the cooler tones of the half-lights and shadows. As a matter of fact the arrangement results in two parallel columns with five values in each column, the lighter tones placed at the right nearest the thumb, grading down to darker tones at the left. One column consists of different values of red, made of mixtures of white with vermilion and lake in varying proportions; a light yellow, made of yellow ochre and white, is placed at the extreme right for the highest lights. The other column consists of a series of neutral tones of varying values, grading down almost to black; they are made of mixtures of red, yellow, and blue (or black in place of the blue) pigments, with white used in varying amounts in the lighter ones.[10] These two columns form the basis for the painting; but other pigments are placed at the side to be used in connection with the other tones. The arrangement of the main part of the palette, but turned into a vertical positon, is shown in fig. 67. Supplementary tones of varying values and hues were mixed up on the palette, but great emphasis is placed, in this as in other books, on the

```
                WT
                Y
            R
            R        N
RO          R   Y    N
(Vermilion) R        N    B
R                    N
(Lake)               N
                BLK
```

FIG. 67. The Palette Described
by Corneille in 1684.

des autres, il est impossible qu'il n'y ait de l'union; car le participation des couleurs contribue beaucoup à l'harmonie d'un tableau, et je pense que c'est ce qui fait dire des tableaux harmonieux qu'ils semble avoir été faits d'une seule palette." (*Essai sur les principes de la peinture*, par Jean Restout, peintre ordinaire du roi, Louis XV; publié avec des notes par A.-R. R. de Formigny de la Londe; Caen, 1863.)

[10] This probably resulted in a warm neutral — that is, slightly toward OY as compared with a mixture of white and black.

necessity of keeping the paint as fresh as possible, the subtler mixtures being made as far as possible by juxtaposing tones on the brush and leaving them undisturbed when applied to the canvas.

All this bears testimony to an extremely careful preparation of the tones on the palette; and all through the eighteenth century and into the nineteenth century, painters continued to prepare their palettes in this painstaking way, as long as the workshop tradition lasted. The final loss of this tradition was due partly to the fact that painters, as well as the general public, which in the course of the nineteenth century developed into an extensive but undiscriminating patron and critic of the arts, became obsessed with the idea of literal imitation as the end of all art; partly to the supplanting of the older manner of training the artist as an apprentice in the workshop of a master, with the modern art-school training. In France, the break came rather suddenly with the suppression of the old French academy by David. It must be remembered that the old academy of the seventeenth and eighteenth centuries was very different from the modern academy. It was more like a medieval guild. Formal instruction in the academy was confined to drawing and occasional lectures. The practice of painting was learned in the workshop of the master as in the earlier Renaissance. The academy stood for tradition, at times somewhat narrow, no doubt, but nevertheless almost indispensable, unless something can be found to take its place. Some, at any rate, of the advantages of that tradition may be recovered by a rational education of the artist in a thorough understanding of the limitations and the possibilities of the terms by means of which he must express his ideas, and of the general principles which govern their use.

9

CONCLUSION — THE USE OF DIFFERENT MODES IN RECENT PAINTING

The foregoing is intended as a brief account of the terms of drawing and painting and the different ways in which they may be used in representation. Its amplification may properly be left to the individual reader on the basis of his past or his future experience. What has been said here is aimed to make the various kinds of painting and drawing intelligible — readable — and thus to form a primary foundation for sound critical judgment in regard to quality, for such judgment can only be arrived at by first of all understanding the point of view and the methods of expression of the artists themselves.

It should be evident from what has been said above that painting is a flexible language for the expression of all sorts of facts and ideas about things which we see; that the conception of drawing and painting as a purely imitative, literal rendering of the appearance of things, which during the last hundred years has almost been taken for granted by most people, is a very limited one, and that much of the finest painting of the past has been based upon entirely different conceptions. If we were to consider painting merely as a matter of correct and exact rendering of the look of things, we should naturally have to regard Byzantine and Romanesque and all Eastern painting as indeed childish or barbaric, and we could then look upon the history of European painting, from Giotto down, as one long, though somewhat broken, glorious progress toward a complete achievement in the literal renderings of the nineteenth century, of which there had been only occasional suggestions in the work of earlier centuries. This has in fact been the point of view taken, though with frequent misgivings, by many writers on art — even Vasari, if not at times Leonardo himself, took something of this attitude when it came to conscious theorizing about art. Moreover, this is actually the implied assumption on which the training of the painter in the regulation art schools has been based for the last hundred years. From this standpoint, furthermore, it would be only reasonable to conclude that all the artists who can in any way be classed as "modernist" are either ignorant or else wilfully inexpert and childlike.

It may perhaps be worth while, in conclusion, to examine this modern art, using the term broadly to include so-called Post-Impressionism and all that has followed, and to try to understand what it is driving at, for it has returned to a use of abstract modes or of hybrid combinations of them in what is to many people a very puzzling fashion.

Looking back into the nineteenth century, it is evident that what the majority of people wanted when they bought pictures — I shall not attempt here to discuss the importance of patronage in connection with the quality of artistic production, or why the controlling patronage of the nineteenth century was peculiarly lacking in discrimination — what the public as a whole wanted was recognizable likeness to the appearance of things, versimilitude, and this the artists and art schools set out to give them.

Of course all artists recognized to some extent that there was more than this matter of verisimilitude involved in really fine painting, but it was a small minority of them, now usually grouped together broadly as the Impressionists, who reacted more definitely against the popular and academic assumptions, though still practicing a strictly naturalistic type of painting. It was men like Manet, Renoir, Monet, Degas, Whistler, and Cézanne, who placed the emphasis on the rendering of the essential organization of tone relations and on design, as has been suggested in our discussion of the mode of the total visual effect, and who, to stress these more important matters, tended to suppress interest in mere subject matter — to do some of their best painting, in fact, in still-life subjects, even of dead fish or cuts of beef, the interest of which was entirely incomprehensible to the ordinary public. Almost all of these painters reacted against the narrow teaching of the nineteenth-century art school or academy and returned first of all to a study of the masterpieces of Renaissance and Baroque painting. Since the workshop traditions had been lost, their painting technique was different; but the more interesting character of their work, as opposed to the imitative rendering of more popular artists, depended largely on this study of earlier painting. The expression of space in Cézanne's work, for example, depended very much on an arbitrary distinguishing of planes based on principles derived from painters like Bellini, Titian, and Poussin. The devices of these earlier painters he often exaggerated so that at times it would almost seem that he had studied Chinese landscape painting. He also exaggerated the principle of uniformity of measure and shape in the brush stroke which he found a striking characteristic of earlier painting. At times he seems to have distorted form wilfully from the point of view of perspective for the sake of an emphasis on two-dimensional pattern while rendering space in an arbitrary fashion. Sometimes, as might be expected since he was constantly experimenting, he didn't seem quite sure of what he was doing and left canvases more or less unfinished when he didn't know how to proceed further without disturbing what interesting quality he had obtained. Naturally there were at the time not many critics or patrons who understood his aims.

In Cézanne, as in Manet and Degas, we find principally a return to the Renaissance for an understanding of methods of expression and of design. It was only natural that other artists, following actually the lead of connoisseurs, collectors, and students of art history, should go farther back to a study of still more abstract methods of expression to be found in so-called primitive art of all kinds. They went back first to the early Renaissance, to the Gothic and Romanesque, to Japanese prints which had been imported into Paris in the fifties (the Impressionists got ideas from these, too), and then to earlier Japanese and Chinese and Indian and Persian art, and finally to the art of Africa, of Pre-Columbian America, and the Oceanic Islands. They recognized the great aesthetic significance of much of this art and they found that it was based on ideas entirely different from those underlying what they had been taught in the art schools. They discovered that in all this art, much of which was obviously finer in many ways than anything they were producing, there was practically nothing of literal rendering of the superficial appearance of things. It was usually abstract in its method — that is, it was in the mode of line and local tone, or possibly in the mode of relief. It was distinctly imaginative and expressional, rather than imitative. Its technique was based on the use of a regular vocabulary of strokes or of tones, learned in each case from preceding masters. The strokes of this vocabulary were frequently abstract and used in calligraphically ornamental or in expressionistic fashion. All this they observed, sometimes in rather a superficial way, occasionally with deeper insight; but in any case their work was affected by it in a more and more revolutionary fashion.

It must be remembered that much of this primitive and abstract art, usually decorative in primary intent, was actually now to be seen exhibited on the walls of museums or of collectors' houses, entirely separated from its original setting — if not in actual fragments, at least in a fragmentary state from the standpoint of its primary environment. Moreover drawings — frankly unfinished studies — were exhibited enframed as complete works of art. The museums, furthermore, showed examples of decorative paintings, of textiles, tiles, and so on, mounted and exhibited as independent works, treated as examples of "pure design," of "pure drawing and painting," although they certainly were not that in the first place.

All these things that the artist saw in the works exhibited in the museums he enthusiastically set out to embody in his own work. He sought for distortion — non-naturalism — more or less for its own sake, often not stopping to consider the very definite reason for the distortion in the medieval or ancient original. He avoided accurate perspective rendering in order to emphasize two-dimensional pattern. He painted in abstract modes — again a revolt against commonplace naturalism. He sought for expressionism — at least something that would look like expressionism as observed in Oriental or medieval art, and for calligraphic touch. Out of the influence of the museum and the collector there developed a cult of the fragmentary — seen perhaps even more in sculpture than in painting — and a cult of the unfinished sketch as something that had a more immediate appeal than a finished performance. Artists now made drawings that actually looked off-hand something like the studies of Renaissance masters, although they might have nothing further in the way of a finished composition in mind themselves, and hastened to set them up in frames as complete works of art. Finally they did not hesitate to produce "decorative" paintings to be regarded as independent complete things, although often these lack the primary demand of the object to be decorated, and inevitably suggest the lines of the music-hall song, "All dressed up and no place to go!"

It is the museum's and the collector's manner of exhibiting things which had much to do, doubtless, with the development some forty years ago of the idea of pure design, or pure drawing and painting, as a means of arriving at a somewhat new point of view in painting, on the assumption, perfectly proper theoretically perhaps, that there might be painting without either representational or decorative intent. It is an idea that has been experimented with in literature as well as in painting, and it illustrates to what extreme point of intellectualism and abstraction persons interested in the arts are willing to go in their new curiosity about non-naturalistic and (to borrow a term from Max Eastman) [1] uncommunicative possibilities. We treat as finished works of art things which in any other age would be thought of as studies or experiments in technical method.

From the standpoint of mode of representation there is something in the whole modern movement that recalls the breakdown of the plastic tradition of classical art and the mingling of Western and Eastern ideas in Early Christian and Byzantine and Romanesque art. As suggested earlier, although tending toward the mode of line and local tone with its emphasis on monumental decoration of architectural surfaces, this art never lost entirely the effects of its derivation from plastic art of the ancient world and so may be regarded as more or less hybrid in character. In the art of the modern movement as a whole there has been a similar breaking down of plastic tradition, although this time more of a conscious reaction against the overimitative art of the nineteenth century, and a similar, though again conscious, hybrid mingling of Eastern and Western points of view.

The general idea of line and local tone and of calligraphic or expressionistic use of line was suggested by Japanese and Chinese painting or by early European painting which itself owed much to the East. At times this mode has been used fairly consistently, at other times the mode of relief; often there has been a hybrid mixing of these two modes, or a mixing of these with other modes. As in Byzantine and Romanesque painting, light and shade is often reduced to the role of superficial pattern and is regarded or disregarded in different parts of the same composition according to exigencies of design and expression. Van Gogh, for example, has given us some paintings that are practically

---

[1] "The Cult of Unintelligibility," *Harper's Magazine*, April, 1929.

line and local tone; in others, he has, like Gauguin and Matisse, introduced elements of light and shade largely for the sake of greater interest in design or for the differentiation of planes in space. The idea of line and local tone he apparently obtained from a study of Japanese prints, some of which he copied in oil. From these he also got the idea of uniformity of shape character, as in the repetition of the cusp-like strokes in his painting of "L'Arlésienne." Matisse has at times used a mode of line and flat tone suggesting the study of Persian painting; but he has introduced occasional areas of tone suggested by light and shadow when he has seen fit to do so.[2] Other painters seem to have striven definitely for the effect obtained in Italian painting of the fifteenth century; or they have mixed the modes in all sorts of ways. In technique, however, as early Christian painting employed the methods handed down from Greek and Roman painting, so these modern painters, both the so-called Post-Impressionists and those more recent, employ for the most part the technique handed down from the nineteenth century. It is principally the method of oil painting and the way of using the brush in rather broad strokes, adopted by the Impressionist painters. Superficially, therefore, the best of this modern painting has a character all its own, and, as in the case of early Christian, Byzantine, and Romanesque painting, this depends on the special circumstances under which it has been evolved. This fact accounts for much of the novel fascination and charm in some of the recent painting. If one appreciates the nature of its development and the different kinds of painting it is directly emulating or combining in somewhat new ways, there is no difficulty in understanding it — in reading it, and finally in evaluating it as one would other kinds of painting. This applies not only to the use of more arbitrary modes of representation but also to experiments in so-called "abstract" art (or pure drawing and painting) of all kinds and also to surrealism in which the objects represented are supposedly only subconsciously related. Although an extraordinary amount of somewhat mystifying nonsense has been written about this art — sometimes it would seem intentionally to endow the many less successful examples with an attractive glamour — about the thing itself there is no mystery whatsoever. Its final value depends on the same

[2] In many cases these variations of tone suggested by effect of light and shadow count in the painting only as changes in local tone.

fundamental principles which determine the value of any art, and it is to be judged accordingly.

Perhaps in the long run the main achievement of the painters of the last seventy years will prove to be the recovery of a concern for the formal and expressive possibilities of the visual or painting terms themselves and of their arrangement in the picture plane or picture surface, for with the exaggerated emphasis on imitative or photographic rendering in the so-called academic art of the nineteenth century this had largely been lost sight of. At least we have again become conscious of this as one of the factors involved in what we think of as good painting. The principal difficulty with much of the more or less abstract painting that has been produced in recent years is that when enclosed within the limits of a frame like an independent picture, without function as enrichment of a particular surface, it is, however perfect, often meager in interest — in manifestation of order — as compared with the richness of organization we find in what we think of as fine examples either of representation or pure pattern.

APPENDIX

I

DESIGN IN TONE RELATIONS

INTRODUCTORY

Although the present volume is intended primarily as a consideration of the principles underlying representation in drawing and painting, it has been necessary to discuss the general theory of tone or color at considerable length and so it seems advisable to conclude with a chapter on design so far as it applies to tone relations and thus to complete the discussion of the general subject of tone or color. Design in space relations, especially as it applies to pictorial composition, may then be left for discussion in a separate work.

That all design is fundamentally a matter of order or organization of some sort is fairly generally accepted. Elsewhere [1] I have attempted to show that aesthetic experience is a question of reaction to emotionally, as well as intellectually, appreciable order, and that the relative value of different aesthetic experiences depends on the quantity and perfection of this appreciable order; also that two things are ordinarily necessary for this emotional experience: first, definite order or organization, and secondly, some element of diversity or disorder, which serves as a means to emphasize the elements of order, and without which the order would seem obvious or monotonous, and uninteresting. The exact amount of diversity necessary can ordinarily be predicted only rather vaguely, but the matter of organization, at least in simpler examples, is perfectly tangible: we can be fairly definite about that, and approximately accurate in any given circumstance about the requirement of diversity.[2]

In applying this to the matter of tone relations we come upon one of the most difficult problems in the whole realm of the arts, and one which is very imperfectly understood. In general, persons who have what we think of as good taste are apt to agree fairly well in the face of specific examples as to what is "good color" and what is "bad color,"

[1] "A Quantitative Theory of Aesthetic Values," *Art Studies*, vol. III (Cambridge, Mass., 1925), p. 133.
[2] Briefly the problem of design or composition may be thought of as a matter of achieving as much organization as possible within the diversity inherent in the original concept. Perfection depends on a maximum of organization combined with a minimum of diversity for the particular concept. Total value may be said to depend first, on the degree of perfection in this relation of order and diversity, and second, on the quantity of order achieved.

although the effect on their taste of changing fashions and habits must always be discounted. On the other hand, when it comes to the reasons for these judgments, the ordinary explanations or prescriptions are not very satisfactory.

It has often been thought that there must be some virtue in certain intervals of hue, as there is mathematical harmony in certain relations of intervals in sound; and all sorts of theories, even including major and minor chords, have been worked out on a basis of the most superficial analogies with musical harmony. As a matter of fact, although the same general principles of design apply to arrangements of both sound tones and visual tones, the specific application is entirely different; for sound tones not only have extension in time instead of in space, but they are distinguished as separate tones when they are overlapped — that is, played at the same time; whereas visual tones, which have extension in two-dimensional space, are destroyed by overlapping and give way to entirely new ones. The juxtaposition of tones in painting involves an entirely different application of the principles of design from what we find in music.

Most books that have been written on the subject of design indicate a failure to appreciate the complexities of the subject of tone or color design; they seem to imply that one or two simple rules might be evolved which would solve the whole problem. Thus certain writers emphasize the possible harmony to be derived from the use of low intensities; others emphasize the possible dominance of one hue region with perhaps the use of small amounts of complementary hues to afford relief or stimulate interest. Still others suggest that all good tone design depends on a balancing of hues and intensities around a neutral center, as if in a satisfactory composition all the tones would average on neutral if they could be spun in proper proportions on a color top. This method has actually been suggested as a means of ensuring good tone design, as if this were the whole thing. One does not have to look far to find splendid examples of tone design which do not average on neutral at all, but which obviously illustrate other methods of achieving tone harmony. As a matter of fact there are a great many different ways of achieving ordered arrangement in the tones of a composition, and of maintaining at the same time the necessary contrast or diversity to make this interesting — that is, emotionally appreciable. These possibilities may be used singly or perhaps in combination according to circumstance.

It is proposed in this section to indicate briefly the principal possibilities in the way of ordered arrangement of the different tonal factors of value, hue, and intensity — not to suggest them as rules that *must* be used in good tone design, but as methods that *may* be used according to circumstance. In practice it is a very complicated affair, for not only are we often satisfied with an approximation to a definite organization of tone, as long as we can feel the intention clearly, but often the tonal arrangement of a composition has to be bent deliberately to the exigencies of spatial design or of expression, in which case the final organization is so complex that it may defy exact analysis in any of its parts. Furthermore there are, I believe, possibilities in the way of tone harmony that are not yet fully understood. Toward the end of the chapter there will be found some suggestions in regard to harmony obtained by uniformity of attraction and by uniformity of hue and intensity contrasts which have, I believe, not been made before except partially in my pamphlet, *Tone Relations in Painting*.[3] Further investigation will be necessary before we may have anything like a complete understanding of the subject.

THE PRINCIPLES OF DESIGN

Dr. Ross has shown that the various manifestations of order in design may be classified in three main general categories. In his different books [4] he varied the terminology used to indicate these categories or principles of order, and other writers have used a great variety of terms usually without much attempt to classify them in a definite way. In this book I shall designate these principles of order as *harmony*, *sequence*, and *balance*.

By *harmony* is meant uniformity of any sort in the different parts of a composition, using the latter term in a very general sense; especially uniformity in which there is no definite feeling of change or movement, or definite feeling of opposition.

By *sequence* is meant uniformity in change or movement, producing a definitely felt progression; especially where there is uniformity or uniform change in the steps or differences between the separate parts of a series. The movement or change may be gradual or alternating. In the latter case it may be called rhythm.

By *balance* is meant uniformity in opposition of any sort.

All design may be regarded as an application of these principles to an arrangement of the terms of a particular art. It has been shown that, in drawing and painting, the terms are partly spatial — position, measure, and shape — and partly tonal — value, hue, and intensity. Consideration of the application of these principles to spatial relations must be left for more extended and separate treatment. Also, I shall not attempt to consider why only under proper circumstances does the perception of order result in aesthetic reaction. For present purposes I shall only attempt to outline briefly the principal possibilities in the way of an application of the principles of order to tone relations.

[3] Cambridge, Mass., 1922.
[4] *Op. cit.*

HARMONY OF VALUES, HUES, AND INTENSITIES

We may in the first place have harmony of value where all the tones of a composition are of exactly the same value, though perhaps varying in hue and intensity. If all the tones are on the whole light, within the limits from HLt to LLt, for example; or on the whole dark, within the limits perhaps from HD to LD; or on the whole middling, within the limits perhaps from LLt to HD; there will be relative or approximate harmony as opposed to the lack of it in a range of values from Wt to Blk. This may be illustrated by holding pieces of paper over portions of the tones in Chart V and leaving only two or three adjacent horizontal rows visible. There is obviously an approximation to uniformity of value in the tones left visible, as compared with the variety of value in the whole chart. This relative harmony of value is as a rule of greater importance in design than absolute uniformity of value. It will be found an important element in the design of many of the finest specimens of Persian textiles, for example.

We may have absolute harmony of hue when all the tones of a composition are of exactly the same hue, although varying possibly in value and intensity; or we may have relative harmony of hue if the tones of a composition are on the whole reddish, or on the whole yellowish, or on the whole bluish, or come within any relatively limited range of hue as compared with the variety of hue in the whole circle. This may be illustrated in Chart V by covering over all but a few of the vertical rows of the chart.

Harmony of intensity may also be absolute, if all the tones in a composition are exactly the same distance from neutral; or it may be relative, if all the tones in a composition are relatively low in intensity, or relatively high in intensity as compared with the complete range. This is illustrated, though only approximately, along the vertical rows in Chart IV.

Under ordinary circumstances a great variety of values, hues, and intensities will seem chaotic and disorderly; on the other hand, great uniformity may seem monotonous and hence valueless artistically. Good designers, therefore, are constantly relieving uniformity of one factor by relative diversity in one or both of the other factors; or, the other way round, introducing a harmony of one factor to compensate for diversity in the others. Thus in much Persian painting it will be found that tones that are strongly contrasted in hue are of the same or nearly the same value, especially if they are juxtaposed, while the strong value contrasts present little contrast of hue and intensity. In a similar way in the Italian painting of the fourteenth and fifteenth centuries, where rather large fields of fairly intense color are often used for decorative surface effect, there is little emphasis on contrasts of light and dark, whereas Leonardo's extreme emphasis on contrasts of light and dark is accompanied by a wise suppression of hue and intensity contrasts. Caravaggio, and Ribera, and Rembrandt also suppress hue and intensity contrasts as they emphasize contrasts of light and shade. On the other hand, some of the worst tone design produced in the whole range of European painting, outside of the nineteenth century, is found in the works of some sixteenth-century painters who tried to combine the older decorative color with the light and shade of Leonardo.

Above we have outlined the possibilities of harmony in each of the three main factors of tone taken singly. We may of course have absolute or approximate harmony of all three factors together, or of any

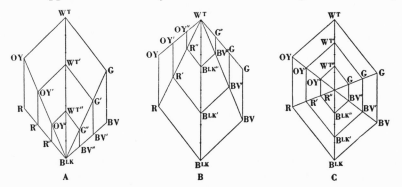

FIG. 68. Harmonization by Reduction of Contrasts of Value and Intensity.

two factors without regard to the third factor. In the latter case we may use diagrams to illustrate some of the principal possibilities.

In the case of absolute harmony of value, hue, and intensity, the result is monotony, which may, in some cases, be important in a single field but is of no significance in a whole composition. But approximate harmony of value, hue, and intensity, where all the tones come within a relatively small part of the whole tone solid, may be of considerable significance. Approximate harmony of two factors, with a relatively wider range in the third factor, is still more important, and may be conveniently expressed in two-dimensional diagrams. Thus, given the tones R, OY, Wt, G, BV, and Blk, as indicated in fig. 68 A, they may be harmonized more or less definitely by pulling them all toward Blk a smaller or greater distance. A common element of relative blackness will be introduced into all of the tones marked ', and still more strongly into all of the tones marked ". The possibility of similar harmonization toward Wt is shown in fig. 68 B; toward neutral-middle in fig. 68 C.

Exercises in which the tones are produced in a composition, first without harmonization, and then with harmonization in the different manners shown, will be found most helpful in illustrating the various possibilities of value and intensity harmony. Examples in nature will be found in the modeling of objects toward blackness in shadow, or their darkening as night comes on, their change toward Wt in reflected lights, or toward neutral gray in mist or fog.

Various possibilities of harmony of hue and intensity are illustrated in figs. 69 and 70. Given the tones R, OY, G, and BV, as in fig. 69, they may be harmonized by pulling them all toward N in varying degrees, as in fig. 69 A, toward Y, as in fig. 69 B, or toward VR, as in fig. 69 C, without changing their relative contrasts with each other. Exercises

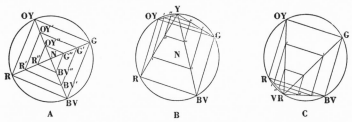

Fig. 69. Harmonization by Reduction of Contrasts of Hue and Intensity.

with actual tones are helpful to illustrate more clearly the possibilities of harmonization indicated in these diagrams also. Good examples in nature are to be found in harmonization under the influence of different colored lights, corresponding approximately to the changes indicated in the diagrams.

In most Venetian painting of the sixteenth century there is a distinctly golden tonality.[5] If what tells as white in a painting by Titian, for example, is compared with the Wt of white paper held in front of it, the white in the painting will be found to be in reality rather decided orange-yellow. It tells as Wt only in relation to the general tonality of the whole picture. By careful opposition of warm and cool tones, Titian makes his blues tell as very rich tones; but on being compared with intense blues, they are found to be as a matter of fact very low in intensity. The harmony of tonality in such a painting is perhaps best expressed in a diagram as in fig. 70 A, or perhaps better in fig. 70 B. Although there is relative expression of practically all the hues in the hue circle, there is actually used only a very limited range of hues and in-

[5] This is of course frequently exaggerated by the yellowing of oil and varnish in the course of time; but originally many of the paintings were probably decidedly golden in tone, made so, very likely, to harmonize with heavy gilded moldings used as enframements in the architectural decoration of the sixteenth century.

tensities, as compared with the whole hue and intensity circle. It is common in such painting to make neutral, obtained by a mixture of white and black pigments, tell as relatively blue. In this case a mixture of red and neutral will tell as violet. Many paintings of the Renaissance, although expressing relatively warm and cool tone, contain no positively cool tones at all. No green or blue pigments are employed in producing them. Some of Rembrandt's portraits are good examples.[6]

Other possibilities in the way of limited ranges of hues and intensities are suggesetd in fig. 70 C and D. The former approximates the

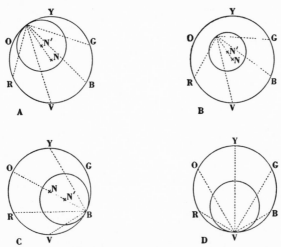

FIG. 70. Use of Limited Ranges of Hue and Intensity.

harmony of bluish tonality found in some of Turner's water-color paintings on blue-gray paper. Fig. 70 D indicates a possible violet tonality. There are almost infinite possibilities in the way of achieving harmony of tonality by the use of such limited ranges of hues and intensities, without the sacrifice of relative diversity. They can be applied to painting either in the manner of representation or in that of pure design.

A diagram like that shown in fig. 21 may be used, as explained on page 19, to indicate harmony of values and hues without regard to the question of intensities. The plotting of the tones of a fine textile, for example, will frequently reveal much of the secret of the tone harmony which it contains, by showing a surprisingly limited range of values. A limited range of hue, from R to Y, for example, or from perhaps O

[6] This question has also been considered in Chapter 7 in connection with the abstract rendering of hue relations.

to G, might also be exhibited clearly in this sort of diagram; but, as a rule, hue must be considered along with intensity, and this diagram is not as useful as the others already described.

In any composition the contrast of each tone with the adjacent tone or tones exerts a definite attraction on the eye of greater or less power. If the attractions exerted by the tone contrasts in all the different parts of the composition are the same, there will be uniformity of attraction over the whole surface of the composition, resulting in a generally harmonious surface. This is an important consideration in all kinds of tone design. Fine and striking examples are to be found in Coptic textiles. Individual specimens vary in the strength of the attractions exerted by their design themes; but in any one the same force of attraction is maintained over the whole surface of the composition.

Another kind of harmony of attraction, which, so far as I know, has not been at all adequately discussed up to the present time, is obtained by achieving a uniformity of attraction of the tones employed in a composition, regardless of their distribution. The simplest possible illustration of this may be made by placing four or five different tones of equal area on a black ground tone, allowing the black to show on all sides of each of the other tones. If the tones are, let us suppose, O–LLt, YG–Lt, GB–M, B–HD, and VR–D, the VR will make the least contrast with the Blk of the ground and will exert the least attraction of all the tones; the attraction of the B will be somewhat greater; that of the GB still greater; and that of the O and the YG greatest of all. There will be no uniformity of attraction, and practically no harmony of any kind in the tone arrangement. If, however, without changing in any way their values, hues, and intensities, the relative sizes of the different areas are changed, by cutting in with the Blk over the B, GB, YG, and O areas, the quantity of each of these other areas may be reduced until it exerts on the eye the same attraction as the larger quantity of the VR. Uniformity of attraction will then be achieved, and there will be a harmony in the whole arrangement entirely absent before. Curiously enough, this change in the quantity relations of the different areas will frequently almost make one believe that the quality of the individual tones has been changed.

As it takes some experience, even in this simple exercise, to achieve perfect uniformity of attraction, the working out of problems in harmony of attraction is excellent as a means of training the eye in sensitiveness of reaction. The same exercise may be carried out on different ground tones. The relative quantities of the different tones will vary according to the contrasts made with the ground tone. If, for example, the tones cited above are placed on a Wt ground, the YG area will be largest, the O somewhat smaller, the GB and B still smaller, and the VR smallest of all. On an OY–Lt ground, the O and YG would be the larger areas, and the others would be much smaller, though just how much smaller must be determined by actual eye judgment.[7]

This is the principle underlying the whole question of quantities — how much of each tone to use in a given composition. It seems to be a fundamental principle in much tone design. When there is a common ground tone, the problem is comparatively simple. Good and striking examples are to be found in many Persian textiles, and in the stained-glass windows of the twelfth and thirteenth centuries, in which the tones are all placed against the dark of the leads and the surrounding iron and stone enframement. The latter are also good examples of the other type of harmony of attraction referred to above.

When the tones are all juxtaposed, instead of isolated against a ground tone, and especially where limited tonalities are employed, the problem is much more complicated, but the end sought is the same. Values, hues, and intensities, together with quantities, may be so adjusted that the different tones attract the eye approximately with the same force. There is practically no difference in principle. As in the case of harmony of value, or hue, or intensity, an approximation to uniform attraction will, in some cases, serve to express the idea of harmony and satisfy the eye almost as well as absolute uniformity. It will depend more or less on the general nature of a composition just how exact the equality must be.

The possibility of a gradation of force in the attractions of the tones of simple patterns will be discussed under the heading of sequence.

HARMONY OF HUE AND INTENSITY CONTRASTS

Another way of achieving a definite organization in tone relations might be spoken of as a harmony of hue and intensity contrasts. If exactly the same intensities of different hues are used, placed against a neutral ground tone, there will be a definitely appreciable harmony in

---

[7] Bradley (Morton C. Bradley, Jr., "A Theory of Tone Attraction," *Technical Studies in the Field of the Fine Arts*, Fogg Museum of Art, Cambridge, Mass., Vol. II, 1933, p. 3) has suggested that to obtain equal attraction of any two tones against a ground tone the quantities must vary inversely to the cube of the contrasts. At least as a starting point this works very well in practice; but even in simple examples the contrast with near or adjacent tones has an effect which is apt to upset any exact mathematical formula. This is especially true if some or all the tones are juxtaposed instead of having the background showing on all sides of each one. In such a case the final adjustment has necessarily to be made by eye. Aside from this, in many cases an approximation will probably be satisfactory, especially in complicated examples like stained glass for instance, so long as the intention can be felt.

the equality of the contrasts between the background and each of the colored tones. This is indicated in fig. 71.

The same principle seems to apply if the ground tone is changed to a definite hue, say OY of a low intensity, as in fig. 72.[8] If on this ground tone are placed tones all at the same distance in hue and intensity from the ground tone, there will be a definite uniformity of contrast in hue and intensity between the different superposed tones and the ground tone; and this seems to be visually appreciable as a definite, but, off-hand, inexplicable harmony. I have never seen this particular possibility referred to in any book on design, but I have had students experiment with the idea with very definite results. It

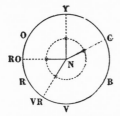

FIG. 71. Harmony of Hue and Intensity Contrasts with Neutral Ground Tone.

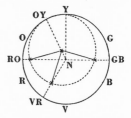

FIG. 72. Harmony of Hue and Intensity Contrasts with Colored Ground Tone.

first occurred to me in connection with a fragment of a Persian carpet in the Boston Museum, where there seemed to be just this definite uniformity of snap of hue and intensity contrast between all the superposed tones and the ground. Some such principle is probably involved in compositions in which there is juxtaposition of the tones instead of a superposition on a uniform ground, but the problem becomes much more involved in this case. Further investigation along this general line, however, may enable us to discover a more definite principle that may be applied in such compositions than the mere matter of harmonization within a limited range of hue and intensity.

What has been said above will at least suffice to outline some of the principal possibilities in connection with the application of the principle of harmony to tone relations, and to suggest avenues for further speculation and investigation. Unfortunately the subject cannot be discussed in great detail without recourse to illustration in actual color, and for this purpose the adjustment of tones has to be much more accurate than can be achieved in any ordinary method of color printing.

[8] To be perfectly accurate, this ought to be worked out on a circle with exact measures of hue and intensity intervals.

SEQUENCE

The subject of tone sequence may be dealt with in much more summary fashion than that of tone harmony, for it is on the whole more obvious, and examples will occur readily to everyone. Skies, birds' feathers, butterflies' wings, petals of flowers, and leaves of plants, are all familiar examples of regular gradation of value or hue or intensity. Fields in design are also constantly organized by means of a gradation of tone. In borders of all kinds we find familiar examples of regular alternation of tones. It will hardly be necessary therefore to do more than for the sake of completeness list the possibilities with little comment.

We may have either gradual or alternate sequence of value, hue, or intensity, or of any two, or of all three combined.

The tone contrasts and the tone quantities in a composition might be so arranged that there would be a regular gradation of the attractions of the different tones; but that this might make a definite appeal to the observer, the arrangement would have to be very simple. The importance of this form of sequence is, I believe, somewhat problematical, though theoretically it is a possibility. An alternation of attractions is, on the other hand, constantly found in rhythmical progressions.

As objects in nature model from light into shadow, the tones change in the form of a regular sequence, as indicated in fig. 33. The relations of the tones stay exactly the same in the different planes of modeling; but there is a proportional diminution of contrasts that produces a very definite organization in all the tones of a subject which is governed by a simple effect of lighting. The interest of interiors, like those painted by Vermeer and de Hoogh, depends largely on the presence of this definite sequence governing all the tone relations. Still-life subjects, as treated by Western painters, also owe a large part of their interest to the fact that the organization of the tones follows this principle. That is why many of the greatest masters from the seventeenth century down to our own day seem to have got more real fun out of the painting of these than of any other subjects. For the real connoisseur also, the *natures mortes*, like those of Monet and Manet, little known by the general public, are perhaps the most nearly perfect performances of modern painting.

In painting, more or less arbitrary tone sequences established on the palette are of the greatest use in achieving definite organization in the tone relations. These may be used in such a way that the sequences are definitely felt in the resulting composition. OY–Lt, RO–M, and VR–D would be an example of a simple tone scheme in which there is a regular gradation of values and hues. Schemes of this sort, with varying intensities, may be used in pure design. Another simple example would be: Y–HLt, R–Lt, B–LLt, Y–M, R–HD, B–D. In this case there is a repetition of the value and hue relations in two different value registers. YG–HLt, RO–Lt, BV–LLt, YG–M, RO–HD, BV–D would be another similar scheme.

The use of regular sequences in representation has been discussed in a preceding chapter.

BALANCE

Balance in design consists, in its simplest form, in the achievement of an equilibrium in the attraction exerted by the various tone contrasts in a composition on either side of a vertical axis, or around a central point. In one case the balance may be called axial, in the other case, central. If the positions, measures, and shapes, and the tones are arranged in an exact opposition, either on the axis or on the center, as the case may be, the balance is obvious. If, on the other hand, the arrangement of tones does not correspond exactly to the arrangement of the positions, measures, and shapes, but there is at the same time an equality in the total tone attractions on either side of the axis or around the center, the balance may be called occult or irregular. Thus in a symmetrical arrangement of positions, measures, and shapes on either side of a vertical axis, as in some of the medieval or Renaissance paintings representing the Madonna and Saints, in which the measures and shapes of the fields on either side of the axis correspond almost exactly, a certain combination of tones on one side may be offset by an entirely different combination on the other, so long as the total attraction is the same. In many Persian carpets there is no exact correspondence of tones in the pattern on the two sides of the axis, but there is perfect balance of attractions. In a similar way, in asymmetrical arrangements of positions, measures, and shapes, a larger amount of a slight contrast on one side of an axis may produce the same attraction on the eye as that of a very strong contrast, but smaller in measure, on the other side. The general principle of the level holds for balance of tones in this case: the farther the tone contrast is from the axis or from the center, the stronger is its attraction.

The term "balance" may also properly be used in connection with another form of equal opposition or antithesis, where a composition is divided into equal areas of what are on the whole light tones, as compared with others which are on the whole dark. This type of balance is found in many of the later Renaissance landscape paintings. The composition must be fairly simple, and the lights and darks respectively well massed together, in order that the balance may be felt. Different colored fields might also be balanced in this way.

Inasmuch as the relations of hues are naturally expressed in a hue circle, with approximate complementaries opposite, it has been supposed that there must be some virtue in a "balancing" of complementary pairs of hues, or in the adjustment of the tones of a composition in such a way that the average of all taken together should be neutral. In this case the balance would certainly have to be based on the true hue circle obtained by the mixing of light, and not on the approximate hue circle which applies to pigment mixtures. But I have never been able to feel that there was any virtue in attempted arrangements of this sort, or in the compositions cited as good examples of hue balance, which could not be accounted for better on the hypothesis of harmony of attraction or harmony of tonality of some other sort. At any rate, there is no average of grayness in most of the Renaissance paintings; these almost all verge on a more or less golden tonality. Many fine Oriental and Western textiles also have distinct tonalities of various sorts other than neutral.

HARMONY, SEQUENCE, AND BALANCE IN CONNECTION WITH PURITY AND BRILLIANCE

The factors of purity and brilliance should be considered in connection with design; but, at present at least, I have little evidence to offer as to the practical significance of the principles of harmony, sequence, and balance as applied to these factors, as differentiated from a combination of value and intensity. Reference has been made above (p. 32) to harmony of brilliance as a possible explanation of the consistency of quality in the tones used by painters like Monet and Renoir. I believe that harmony of purity among different hues may be involved in the peculiar beauty of quality to be found in the tones of many textiles. So far as I know, little has been done in the way of experimentation on the basis of this idea. However, as has been pointed out earlier, uniformity of purity is a definite factor in the organization of tones as objects model from light into shadow. It is so continually present in all that we see that we take it for granted and we only become conscious of it when it is called emphatically to our attention in painting.

II

THE EMOTIONAL SIGNIFICANCE OF DIFFERENT GENERAL TONALITIES

A discussion of the general subject of color would hardly be complete without some reference to the emotional significance of varying tonalities, or of varying arrangements of tone contrasts. This has to do especially with the possibilities of expression of mood by the deliberate choice of certain ranges of hues, intensities, or values, or by strong or slight contrasts of any of these factors, aside from the matter of arrangement from the standpoint of formal design. It is a matter of common experience that on the stage a yellowish tonality suggests an atmosphere of general cheerfulness, as opposed to the feeling of gloominess often produced by a subdued violetish lighting. Psychologists have conducted experiments to test the emotional reaction to different colored lighting effects, and red has naturally been found exciting, yellow on the whole more cheerful, green restful, and violets and violet-blues comparatively depressing. The ranges of values and of intensities, as well as of hue, would in this case play a part in the general effect. The emotional result is partly a matter of association, but partly also, I suppose, a matter of definite physiological reaction. Many of these variations in reaction to different tonalities seem to be fairly universal, and they may be used to enhance the expression of general mood in painting or in lighting on the stage. Variations in the strength of contrast between the tones in a composition may also have an emotional significance. A more exciting effect is produced by sharply defined contrasts from tone to tone, a more restful effect by gradual transitions. Similar differences of effect may be produced by a breaking-up of the measures of the tones to produce a choppy, lively effect, as opposed to the greater calm and dignity to be obtained in juxtaposition of large and simple masses. The tonal arrangements of a composition may thus be made to emphasize the character of the general conception.

The possibilities of expression suggested above have been used more or less definitely in a great deal of the painting of the past; but in the last few years they have been pushed farther, I believe, in connection with design and lighting on the stage than in painting. As far as I know, the subject has not been very thoroughly studied either in connection with the painting of the past or as to its theoretical possibilities.

III

THE QUESTION OF PREFERENCE FOR
INDIVIDUAL TONES

Investigations have sometimes been conducted in which large numbers of persons have been asked to express their relative preference or dislike for a series of individual tones. It has always seemed to me that in connection with the problem of aesthetic experience the results of these investigations are of little significance, even if it could be shown that they were fairly universal and based on physiological reactions. As a matter of fact many of our simple preferences are founded on merely personal association and prejudice, and, although it may be true that we cannot enjoy very much looking at anything which we associate with a disagreeable event or with a person whom we dislike, still mere agreeableness has little to do with aesthetic experience, except as a possible condition. Ordinary likes and dislikes are transcended by the organization that underlies aesthetic experience of the higher orders. It is possible that popular art, with its short-lived appeal, can hardly afford to be disagreeable — we must have our pretty faces and our happy endings — but art of more lasting value may often be based on motives which are in themselves not at all pleasant. Examples in music and literature will readily occur to anyone. In tone relations in painting the harmony resulting from a definite organization of relationships is of much greater importance than the superficial attractiveness of this or that individual tone. Many persons have what they call their favorite colors or colors which they dislike. Often this depends primarily on what is thought to be becoming to a particular complexion, or on some individual association or experience. Sometimes a prejudice of this sort may be well-nigh universal in a given community for a certain time. Thus in the nineteenth century people were not used to seeing violet tones used very much in painting, and at first they tended to dislike all pictures in which intense violets appeared, or in fact high intensities of any kind. The dislike for violet arose partly from the fact that violet tonality in a picture was apt to be out of harmony with the usual decorative surroundings of the nineteenth century, but it was due largely to unthinking prejudice. To-day we have almost all of us got over our dislike for violetish tones and high intensities in general, when properly used. Sentimental people and those who like to pose as being "artistic" are, of course, apt to pride themselves on their individual preferences, and no doubt our personal leanings by their variety add to the gaiety of life; but, as a general rule, an intelligent person may, if he likes, get over his prejudices in regard to particular hues or tonalities, as he may frequently surmount other prejudices of association which interfere with aesthetic judgment and artistic appreciation.

IV

A HYBRID MODE OF DRAWING AS ILLUSTRATED IN WINCHESTER MSS.

Some years ago when in one of our courses students were asked to make studies after drawings in some of the manuscripts of the Winchester school of the tenth and eleventh centuries, it was necessary to call particular attention to the ordered relationships of lines used to represent the folds of drapery — otherwise they tended to overlook this and to reproduce the sketchy effect of the broken lines while missing the continuity of the edges not obviously defined but nevertheless implicit in the original (Plate LXV). I did not at first understand the reason for the peculiar character of the method of drawing drapery exhibited in these manuscripts, but it finally occurred to me that it could only have come about through a derivation from a way of representing drapery in which there was modeling in light and shadow. In other words it resulted from a gradual transformation of a plastic manner of representation into a linear one, but with line used in quite a different way than it would naturally have been used without plastic antecedents.

Figure 73 may serve as a diagram to show how this transformation came about. In (a) there is a continuous line to show the edge of the fold. This was the natural manner used to delineate drapery forms to be found in Greek vase "paintings" and in Chinese paintings and drawings where in both cases there was simply a linear tradition. (b) shows approximately the way in which folds of drapery were represented in later Greek and Roman painting. When this formula for drapery folds was broken down into a flattish pattern in Byzantine painting the result was similar to that shown in (c). Something like this is to be seen in many Byzantine mosaics. There is now an interruption in the continuity of the zigzag edge while the side and lower edge are in each case made continuous to produce an alternating pattern. Reduced to line we have something like (d), while expressed in the nervous broken line of the Winchester manuscripts it is like (e). The continuity of the zigzag edges of the folds is still carefully preserved, but it is somewhat obscured. Students were apt to overlook the ordered connection of the lines to show this unless their attention was particularly directed to it.

The diagram in fig. 73 is shown here merely to illustrate in skeleton form what happened in the case of the representation of this particular subject matter when the plastic tradition of classical art was gradually broken down. It may be suggestive of a process that occurred in the representation of other subject matter.

This particular manner of drawing of the Winchester manuscripts may very likely have been derived from a more and more sketchy style possibly used in later classical painting. Evidence of such a derivation is to be seen in the drawings of the Utrecht Psalter of the Reims school of the ninth century. The manner of the Winchester manuscripts would in that case be a reduction of such drawing to a more rigid formula.

This seems to account for the peculiar character of much Byzantine and Romanesque painting which differentiates it from that in which, as in the case of most Chinese and Japanese painting, a purely linear tradition was preserved. The Byzantine and Romanesque manners of representation were derived from a disintegration or transformation of the plastic classical manner either into pure delineation similar to that of the Winchester manuscripts or into a flat pattern often difficult to interpret without reference to its plastic antecedents.

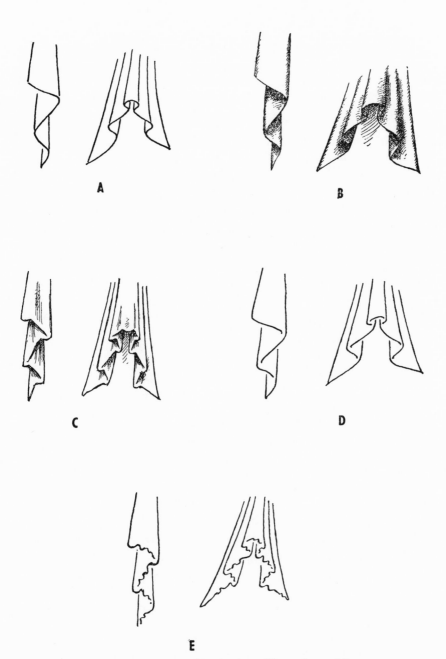

FIG. 73. Schematic Suggestion of Derivation of Byzantine and Romanesque
Manner of Drawing Detail of Drapery.
A. Greek or Chinese Manner.   B. Later Greek or Roman Manner.
C. Byzantine Manner.   D. Reduced to Line.
E. Winchester Manner.

BIBLIOGRAPHICAL NOTE

A list of some of the books and articles about color and the technique of painting which may be found useful in connection with the subject matter of this book is given below. It must be understood that this is not intended to be anything like a complete bibliography. Reference to other books will be found in the text. More extended bibliographies will be found in some of the books mentioned.

The following deal with the general theory of color:

R. M. Evans, *An Introduction to Color* (New York: Wiley, 1948).
    Mr. Evans is head of the color control department of the Eastman Kodak Company, and in this book he reviews our present knowledge about the subject. The discussion of the question of adaptation of the eye to different "brightnesses" and "chromaticities" is of especial interest from the point of view of painting. It may be noted that the matter of purity (as defined herein) is completely ignored.

M. C. Bradley, Jr., "Systems of Color Classification," *Technical Studies in the Field of the Fine Arts*, Fogg Museum of Art, Cambridge, Mass., Vol. VI, No. 4 (April, 1938).

"Report of the Colorimetry Committee of the Optical Society of America, 1920–1921," Journal of the Optical Society of America, Vol. VI, No. 6 (August, 1922).

Chapters from the forthcoming "Colorimetry Report," Journal of the Optical Society of America: Vol. XXXIII, No. 10 (October, 1943); Vol. XXXIV, No. 4 (April, 1944), No. 5 (May, 1944), and No. 11 (November, 1944); Vol. XXXV, No. 1 (January, 1945).

M. Luckiesh, *Color and its Applications* (New York, 1915).

A. H. Munsell, *A Color Notation* (Boston, 1905).

Atlas of the Munsell Color System, The Munsell Research Laboratory, Baltimore.
    For purposes of design where hue and chroma (or intensity) intervals are involved this is very useful. For the more practical purposes of the painter, however, this classification does not work as well as the more approximate one devised by Dr. Ross and set forth in the present book in the form of the working tone or color solid and diagrams derived from this. A defect in the proportions of the Munsell solid is discussed in the text.

E. Jacobson, *The Color Harmony Manual* (Chicago: Container Corporation of America, 1942).
This is based on the Ostwald classification and solid, and consists of small books containing removable tabs of different colors which can be especially useful for matching. The solid itself has little meaning since hues at highest intensity are all placed on the equator regardless of difference of value, and consequently linear distances have no relation to color contrasts. Many of the conclusions as to color harmony are of at least questionable significance.

The following deal more especially with the art of painting:
D. W. Ross, *A Theory of Pure Design* (Boston and New York, 1907).
———, *On Drawing and Painting* (Boston and New York, 1912).
———, *The Painter's Palette* (Boston and New York, 1919).
A. P. Laurie, *The Materials of the Painter's Craft* (London and Edinburgh, 1910).
———, *The Painter's Methods and Materials* (Philadelphia, 1926).
G. L. Stout and R. J. Gettens, *Painting Materials* (New York: Van Nostrand, 1942).
G. L. Stout, *The Care of Pictures* (New York: Columbia University Press, 1948).
The first section of this book contains a useful discussion of the construction of pictures.
Cennino Cennini, *Il Libro dell' Arte*, translation by Christiana J. Herringham (London, 1899); another translation by D. V. Thompson, Jr. (New Haven: Yale University Press, 1933).
Among the earlier treatises on the art of painting this is particularly instructive in its detailed description of the procedures of the fourteenth and fifteenth centuries in Italy.
F. Schmid, *The Practice of Painting* (London: Faber and Faber, 1948).
This book describes the palettes of many different painters as revealed partly in treatises and partly in the representation of palettes in self-portraits and other pictures of artists at work. In these the different pigments are usually laid out along the outer edge and the tones for actual painting mixed with the palette knife in the central space to give sequences approximating what I have described as Type A. Some are simple, others very elaborate. The book is also useful for its bibliography which includes reference to the *Catalogue of the Exhibition of Books on the Practice of Drawing and Painting from 1650 to 1850* (University of London: Courtauld Institute of Art, 1934).

The following deal with aesthetic theory and criticism:

G. D. Birkhoff, *Aesthetic Measure* (Cambridge: Harvard University Press, 1933).

T. M. Greene, *The Arts and the Art of Criticism* (Princeton: Princeton University Press, 1940).

A. Pope, "A Quantitative Theory of Aesthetic Values," *Art Studies*, vol. III (Cambridge: Harvard University Press, 1925).

PLATES

PLATE I

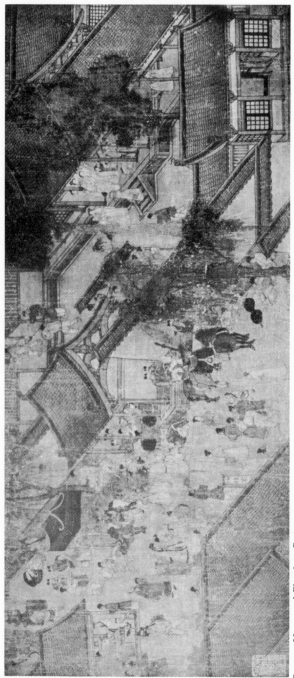

Courtesy Museum of Fine Arts, Boston

THE LADY WEN-CHI'S RETURN TO CHINA, BY A CHINESE PAINTER OF THE SUNG EPOCH

DETAIL OF A LONG ROLL, PAINTED ON SILK

Painting in mode of line and local tone with accurate use of diagonal projection (see p. 54)

STUDY FOR FIGURE OF ADAM
BY ANTONIO POLLAIUOLO (1429–1498)

Pen Drawing

Expression of three-dimensional form by organized relationship and abstract
devices in handling of line (see pp. 59–60, also Plate III)

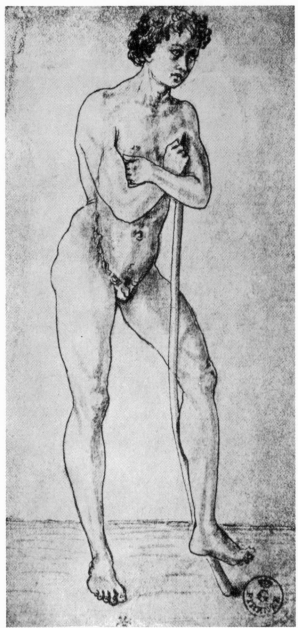

Uffizi Gallery, Florence

STUDY OF FIGURE
BY A PUPIL OR FOLLOWER OF POLLAIUOLO
Pen Drawing
To contrast with Plate IIA (see pp. 59–60)

PLATE III

DETAIL OF PLATE IIA

PLATE IV

Uffizi Gallery, Florence

STUDY FOR FIGURE IN FRESCO IN SISTINE CHAPEL
BY PINTURICCHIO (1454–1513)

PEN DRAWING

Expression of three-dimensional form by abstract devices in handling of line
(see pp. 60–61)

PLATE V

Uffizi Gallery, Florence

STUDY AFTER ENGRAVING BY MANTEGNA
BY RAPHAEL (1483–1520)

PEN DRAWING

Expression of three-dimensional form by abstract devices in the handling
of line (see p. 61)

PLATE VI

FIGURE STUDIES (DETAIL) BY RUBENS (1577–1640)

PEN DRAWING

Expression of three-dimensional form by abstract devices in the handling of line
(see p. 61)

PLATE VII

From *Selected Relics of Japanese Art*

PORTION OF A ROLL REPRESENTING A FANCY PLAY, BY TOBA SOJO (JAPANESE, TWELFTH CENTURY)

Brush Drawing

Expression of three-dimensional form by abstract devices in the handling of line (see p. 61)

PLATE VIII

From *Original Drawings by Rembrandt*   Courtesy Martinus Nijhoff, The Hague

CHRIST IN THE GARDEN (DETAIL)
BY REMBRANDT (1606–1669) OR A PUPIL

PEN AND WASH DRAWING

Expression of three-dimensional form by abstract devices in the handling of line. Perhaps a copy after Rembrandt; but the drawing of the angel is interesting to compare with the drawing of the central rabbit by Toba Sojo, Plate VII (see p. 61)

PLATE IX

EDINBURGH FROM ST. ANTHONY'S CHAPEL, BY J. M. W. TURNER (1775–1851)

PENCIL DRAWING

Distinction of planes by arbitrary selection and suppression of details (see p. 61)

PLATE X

Courtesy Museum of Fine Arts, Boston

PORTION OF LANDSCAPE ROLL, BY TUNG YUAN (CHINESE, SUNG EPOCH)

BRUSH DRAWING

Use of wash and line for distinction of planes forward and back in much the same manner as line is used in the drawing by Turner, Plate IX (see pp. 61-62)

PLATE XI

From *Notes by Mr. Ruskin on Samuel Prout and William Hunt* Courtesy The Fine Arts Society, London

EVREUX
BY SAMUEL PROUT (*c.* 1783–1852)
PENCIL DRAWING
Distinction of planes by arbitrary devices in handling of line (see p. 62)

PLATE XII

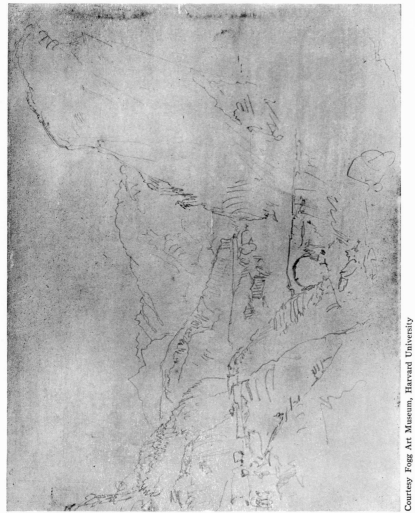

ALPINE VALLEY, BY J. M. W. TURNER (1775–1851)

PENCIL DRAWING

Distinction of planes by arbitrary selection and suppression of details (see p. 62)

PLATE XIII

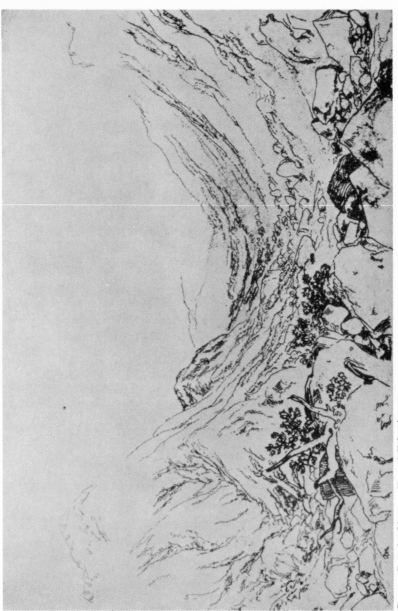

BEN ARTHUR, BY J. M. W. TURNER (1775–1851)

Etched State of Plate from *Liber Studiorum*

Expression of three-dimensional form by abstract devices in handling of line (see p. 62)

PLATE XIV

Courtesy Fogg Art Museum, Harvard University

SOURCE OF THE ARVERON, BY J. M. W. TURNER (1775–1851)

ETCHED STATE OF PLATE FROM *Liber Studiorum*

Except for lower right-hand corner (by Turner's own hand) etching was made by the engraver, probably H. Dawes, after original sketch by Turner. It thus illustrates work of the "school" as opposed to work of the master in Plate XIII (see pp. 62–63). Compare Plates IIa and IIb.

PLATE XV

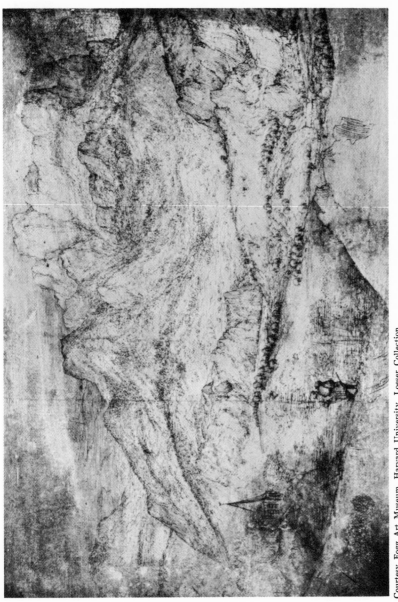

LANDSCAPE BY PIETER BRUEGHEL (?-1569)

PEN DRAWING

Expression of three-dimensional form by deliberate selection and suppression of detail. Compare Tung Yuan and Turner, Plates IX, X, and XII (see p. 63)

PLATE XVI

From *Selected Relics of Japanese Art*

STORM
BY SESSON (JAPANESE, SIXTEENTH CENTURY)
BRUSH DRAWING
Use of abstract line-motives in rendering of organization of form in various
details of landscape (see p. 63)

PLATE XVII

PROCRIS AND CEPHALUS, BY J. M. W. TURNER (1775-1851)

ETCHED STATE OF PLATE FROM *Liber Studiorum*

Use of abstract line motives in rendering of foliage (see p. 64)

PLATE XVIII

Courtesy Fogg Art Museum, Harvard University

ACTOR
BY TORII KIYOMASU
(JAPANESE, EIGHTEENTH CENTURY)
COLOR PRINT
Expressionistic use of line (see p. 65)

PLATE XIX

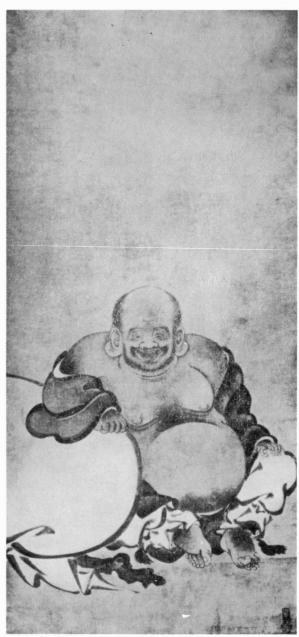

From *Selected Relics of Japanese Art*

HOTEI
BY KANO YUKINOBU
(JAPANESE, SIXTEENTH CENTURY)

Brush Drawing

Expressionistic use of line (see p. 65)

PLATE XX

COURTESAN IN GUISE OF BUDDHIST DEITY OF COMPASSION
BY HARUNOBU (JAPANESE, EIGHTEENTH CENTURY)

COLOR PRINT

Expressionistic use of line (see p. 65)

PLATE XXI

From *Selected Relics of Japanese Art*

BODHISATTVA
BY A JAPANESE PAINTER OF THE TWELFTH CENTURY
PAINTING ON SILK
Expressionistic use of line (see p. 66)

PLATE XXII

Courtesy Museum of Fine Arts, Boston

HEAD OF YOUTH
BY LORENZO DI CREDI (1456–1537)
SILVER-POINT DRAWING
Form drawing (see p. 67)

PLATE XXIII

STUDY OF HEAD
BY MICHELANGELO (1475–1564)
CHALK DRAWING
Form drawing (see p. 67)

PLATE XXIV

Courtesy Museum of Fine Arts, Boston

DEATH OF THE VIRGIN
BY SCHONGAUER (*c.* 1445/50–1491)
LINE ENGRAVING
Form drawing (see p. 67)

PLATE XXV

STUDY
BY REMBRANDT (1606–1669)
PEN AND WASH DRAWING
Form-drawing (see p. 68)

PLATE XXVI

STUDY FOR PAINTING
BY TIEPOLO (1696–1770)
PEN AND WASH DRAWING
Abstract form drawing (see p. 68)

PLATE XXVII

From Fischel, *Raphaels zeichnungen*, pl. 231

STUDY FOR PAINTING (DETAIL) BY RAPHAEL (1483–1520)

Form drawing with organized spacing of lines used in shading (see p. 68)

PLATE XXVIII

ARCHITECTURAL DETAIL
BY A STUDENT
PENCIL DRAWING
Abstract form drawing (see p. 69)

PLATE XXIX

Courtesy The Vasari Society, London

FIGURE STUDY
BY FILIPPO LIPPI (1406–1469)
CRAYON AND WHITE ON GRAY PAPER
Form drawing (see p. 69)

PLATE XXX

Courtesy Fogg Art Museum, Harvard University

RAISING OF LAZARUS
BY REMBRANDT (1606–1669)
Etching
Form drawing with delineation in the lights (see p. 70)

PLATE XXXI

PORTRAIT
BY NANTEUIL (*c.* 1623–1678)
LINE ENGRAVING AFTER PAINTING BY LE BRUN
Color-value drawing (see p. 71)

PLATE XXXII

PORTRAIT OF SNYDERS
BY VAN DYCK (1599–1641)
ETCHING
Color-value drawing on principle of sliding scale (see p. 73)

PLATE XXXIII

From *Degas* by Paul Lafond

STUDY OF MANET
BY DEGAS (1834–1917)
PENCIL DRAWING
Color-value drawing on principle of sliding scale (see p. 73)

PLATE XXXIV

DETAIL OF ROCK-CUT FIGURE AT LUNG MÊN, CHINA
EARLY T'ANG

Expression of details of form by line (see pp. 75–76)

PLATE XXXV

HEAD FROM CHIOS; GREEK, FOURTH CENTURY

Expression of form by plastic modeling of surface with suppression
of sharp contours. Contrast Plates XXXIV and XXXVI (see p. 75)

PLATE XXXVI

DETAIL FROM TYMPANUM, MOISSAC
FRENCH ROMANESQUE, TWELFTH CENTURY
Expression of details of form by line. Compare Plate XXXIV (pp. 75–76)

PLATE XXXVII

San Vitale, Ravenna

Photograph by Alinari

EMPEROR JUSTINIAN AND COURT, BYZANTINE WORK OF SIXTH CENTURY

Mosaic

Painting in hybrid mode — mingling of classical plastic tradition and oriental point of view (see p. 76)

PLATE XXXVIII

FIGURES OF PROPHETS
SPANISH ROMANESQUE PAINTING OF
TWELFTH CENTURY

DETAIL OF DECORATION OF APSE ORIGINALLY IN S. MARIA DE MUR

Painting in hybrid mode, showing survival of classical tradition
in painting essentially in manner of line and local tone

(see p. 76)

PLATE XXXIX

LADIES OF COURT PREPARING NEW SILK, BY HUI T'SUNG (CHINESE, TWELFTH CENTURY)

PORTION OF ROLL PAINTED ON SILK

Painting in mode of line and local tone (see p. 77)

PLATE XL

PORTRAIT
BY CHINESE PAINTER OF MING EPOCH

DETAIL OF PAINTING ON SILK

Painting in mode of line and local tone with variation of tone
to distinguish planes (see p. 77)

PLATE XLI

Courtesy Museum of Fine Arts, Boston

DISCIPLES OF BUDDHA CROSSING A STREAM
BY CHOU CHI-CHANG AND LIN T'ING-KUEI
(CHINESE, TWELFTH CENTURY)

PAINTING ON SILK

Mode of line and local tone with use of abstract line
motives in rendering of water, clouds, and draperies
(see p. 78)

PLATE XLII

LAST SUPPER, BY ANDREA DEL CASTAGNO (*c.* 1410–1457)

FRESCO

Painting in mode of relief (see p. 8o)

PLATE XLIII

Arena Chapel, Padua   Photograph by Alinari, Florence

JOACHIM AND THE SHEPHERDS
BY GIOTTO (1266–1336)

Fresco

Painting in mode of relief. Compare sculpture in relief
by Andrea Pisano, Plate XLIV (see p. 81)

PLATE XLIV

Baptistry, Florence   Photograph by Alinari, Florence

ST. JOHN BAPTIZING
BY ANDREA PISANO (?–1348/49)
DETAIL OF BRONZE DOORS
Compare painting by Giotto, Plate XLIII (see p. 81)

PLATE XLV

Riccardi Palace, Florence   Photograph by Alinari, Florence

JOURNEY OF THE MAGI
BY BENOZZO GOZZOLI (1420–1497)
Fresco (Detail)
Painting in mode of relief; compare sculpture in relief, Plate XLVI (see p. 81)

PLATE XLVI

Baptistry, Florence

SACRIFICE OF ISAAC
BY GHIBERTI (1378–1455)
DETAIL OF BRONZE DOORS
Compare painting, Plate XLV (see p. 81)

PLATE XLVII

MADONNA AND ANGELS BY SPINELLO ARETINO (*c.* 1346–1410)

TEMPERA

Painting in mode of relief without reference to space forward and back (see p. 83)

PLATE XLVIII

ANNUNCIATION
BY ANTONIAZZO ROMANO(?) (ACTIVE 1460–1508)
TEMPERA
Painting in mode of relief (see p. 84)

PLATE XLIX

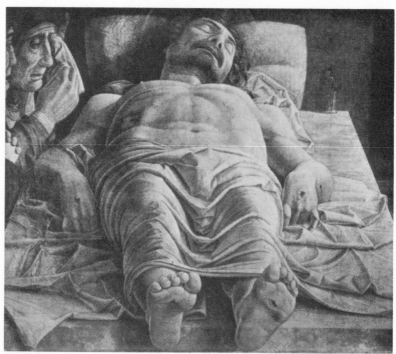

Brera, Milan   Photograph by Alinari, Florence

DEAD CHRIST
BY MANTEGNA (1431–1506)
TEMPERA
Painting in mode of relief with foreshortening as opposed to perspective
(see p. 86)

PLATE L

PORTRAIT
BY PAINTER OF FAYUM, EGYPT
THIRD CENTURY

Encaustic

Painting in hybrid mode — breaking down of classical
plastic tradition (see p. 87)

PLATE LI

MADONNA AND ANGELS
BY MANTEGNA (1431–1506)
TEMPERA (DETAIL OF LARGE ALTARPIECE)
Painting in mode of relief (see p. 87)

PLATE LII

Museum, Berlin   Photograph by Photographische Gesellschaft, Berlin

MADONNA AND SAINTS
BY CRIVELLI (1430/35–*c.* 1495)

TEMPERA

Painting in mode of relief with many details of ornament modeled out
in actual relief (see p. 87)

PLATE LIII

Sistine Chapel, Rome

Photograph B. Braun et Cie., Paris

CREATION OF ADAM, BY MICHELANGELO (1475–1564)

FRESCO

Painting in mode of relief — sculpturesque conception (see p. 87)

PLATE LIV

MIRACLE OF ST. MARK, BY TINTORETTO (1518–1594)

Oil — Venetian Procedure

Painting in Venetian pictorial mode (see p. 89)

PLATE LV

ENTOMBMENT, BY TITIAN (1477–1576)
OIL — VENETIAN PROCEDURE
Painting in Venetian pictorial mode (see p. 89)

Louvre, Paris

PLATE LVI

Courtesy Isabella Stewart Gardner Museum, Boston   Photograph by T. Marr and Son

RAPE OF EUROPA, BY TITIAN (1477–1576)

OIL — VENETIAN PROCEDURE

Painting in Venetian pictorial mode (see p. 90)

PLATE LVII

DRAGONS, BY CH'ÊN JUNG (CHINESE, SUNG EPOCH)

BRUSH DRAWING

Device used for distinguishing planes similar to that used in Titian's Europa, Plate LVI (see p. 90)

PLATE LVIII

Czernin Collection, Vienna

PORTRAIT OF PAINTER
BY VERMEER (1632–1675)
OIL
Painting in mode of total visual effect — "super-reality" (see pp. 93–95 and 99)

PLATE LIX

ARNOLFINI AND HIS WIFE
BY JAN VAN EYCK (c. 1390–1441)
OIL — FLEMISH PROCEDURE
Mode of total visual effect (see p. 96)

PLATE LX

Courtesy National Gallery, London

ST. JEROME BY ANTONELLO DA MESSINA (1430–1479)
OIL — ADAPTATION OF FLEMISH PROCEDURE
Painting in mode of total visual effect (see p. 97)

PLATE LXI

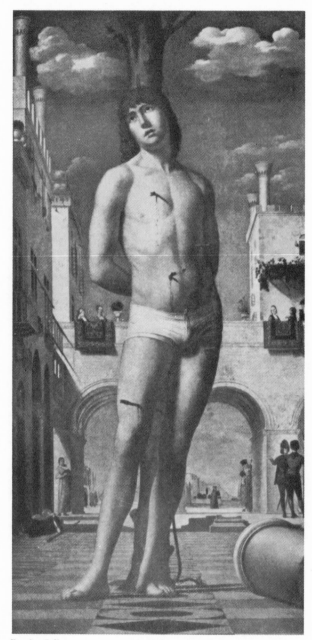

Dresden Gallery   Photograph by F. Bruckmann, Munich

ST. SEBASTIAN
BY ANTONELLO DA MESSINA (1430–1479)
OIL — ADAPTATION OF FLEMISH PROCEDURE
Painting in mode of total visual effect (see p. 97)

PLATE LXII

Dresden Gallery

Photograph by Alinari, Florence

MADONNA AND SAINTS, BY JAN VAN EYCK (c. 1390–1441)

OIL — FLEMISH PROCEDURE

Painting in mode of total visual effect, but without regard for literal effect of light (see p. 97)

PLATE LXIII

Louvre, Paris   Photograph by Braun et Cie., Paris

CHANCELLOR ROLIN KNEELING BEFORE MADONNA
BY JAN VAN EYCK (*c.* 1390–1441)
OIL — FLEMISH PROCEDURE

Painting in mode of total visual effect — telescopic treatment of detail and independent light effects in foreground and landscape (see pp. 97 and 99)

PLATE LXIV

Courtesy Mr. Maurice Wertheim, New York

THE REHEARSAL BY DEGAS (1834–1917)

Oil

Mode of total visual effect with regard for adaptation of the eye — optical effect (see p. 95)

PLATE LXV

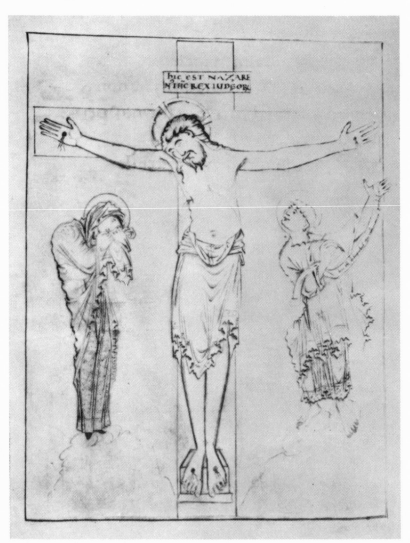

CRUCIFIXION
FROM MANUSCRIPT OF WINCHESTER SCHOOL, TENTH CENTURY
Use of line depending on derivation from plastic tradition of classical art
(see p. 157)

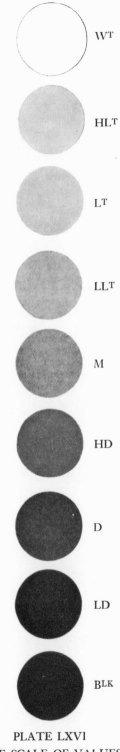

WT

HLT

LT

LLT

M

HD

D

LD

BLK

PLATE LXVI
THE SCALE OF VALUES

A

B

C

PLATE LXVII

DIAGRAMMATIC ILLUSTRATION OF DIFFERENT
WAYS OF RENDERING VALUE RELATIONS

A, normal rendering; B, crowding of the darks;
C, crowding of the lights (see pp. 100–103)